Tales From Behind the Mic

"If you're a music lover, you will love this book. It's a walk thru the history of rock & roll and a peek into the lives of stars who made a lot of it happen. Just a great read!"

– Scott Shannon
CBS-FM New York

Claire Stevens

outskirts press

Outskirts Press, Inc.
http://www.outskirtspress.com

ISBN: 978-1-9772-0814-9

Outskirts Press and the "OP" logo are trademarks belonging to Outskirts Press, Inc.

PRINTED IN THE UNITED STATES OF AMERICA

"I loved it…and anyone who loves music will want to marinate in it…What a remarkable journey you took me on…the "hits" and "misses" of my life were reflected in the stories you tell. You have an amazing ability to weave together the multi-colored tapestry of American music…It is a book full of "friends" and confidants… the musicians who shared the most important parts of my life's journey…I had almost forgotten Ellie Greenwich and many of the others who danced through the days and nights of my youth…It is a book to be read many times over…on quiet nights when sleep comes grudgingly…and the memories of these stories and that music…gets me through the night…Congratulations!

…John (Professor Jonathan B.) Bell
Z-100 Morning Zoo, New York

Thanks for the memories, Claire. It was a hot-rockin' Flame-throwing read!

…JJ Walker
SiriusXM 70s on 7

You laughed with Claire Stevens on New York's Z-100 Morning Zoo for years. Now you can curl up and enjoy her often startling revelations about some of music's biggest icons. Simply put: read this book!

…Brian Wilson
Media host and author

I truly enjoyed this book, especially since I grew up in Brooklyn. My grandmother was best friends with Neil Sedaka's mother!

…Spyder Harrison
SiriusXM Hits 1

FORWARD

Music has always been my life's blood.

As a kid, I lived in New York City, and what a place to be! The top radio stations in the world were right there, broadcasting live — just blocks from my apartment building! WMCA and the Good Guys... WMGM with curly-headed Peter Tripp waiting for me in the third row...rock and rollin' Alan Freed... Murray the "K" Kaufman and his swinging soiree, turning us on to the hippest new pastime of the era, watching submarine races ...William B. Williams playing the Great American Songbook on WNEW-AM...my favorite relative, "Cousin" Bruce Morrow...Howlin' Wolfman Jack...the dynamic icon Dan Ingram...and all the other amazing talents we heard on our AM radios in the car and coming through those little transistors we took to the beach and hid under our pillows at night.

I guess it was no surprise, then, that all my life I wanted to be the disc jockey dropping the needle on those records, and have a jingle with my name in it.

The chance to realize my dream came much later, and so far, has lasted nearly four decades.

After spending 2½ years as news director/anchor and disc jockey at a small Westchester station, my big break came in 1983 when the brilliant programmer, air personality, and multi-honored Hall(s) of Famer Scott Shannon heard my voice. I spent the next eight years at WHTZ (Z-100) in New York, as news director and lone female member of the world-infamous Z-100 Morning Zoo Crew. I also wrote and anchored a daily news report for the Fox Television Network.

My next stop was KOOL 96.7 (WKHL), an Oldies station, where I was the midday disc jockey. It was there I launched a one-hour Sunday night show called *Rockin' Back*™, on which I interviewed many of the incredible artists on our playlist, all of whom were original members of their respective groups. Besides the ones in this book, I spoke to dozens of superstars like Frankie Valli, Ray Manzarek, Eric Burdon, Duke Fakir, Lesley Gore, Paul Anka, members of Chicago and the Spinners, Tony Orlando, Gene Pitney, Felix Cavaliere, Ben E. King, and Martha Reeves.

For a while, I covered Oldies, Urban (R&B), and Adult Standards for a web-based morning prep service. My voice was heard on such prestigious New York City radio stations as WCBS-FM, WMXV (Mix 105), WYNY, WOR, WABC (Network), and WNEW-AM, as well as on the SONY (SW) Worldwide Network, where I was a Smooth Jazz personality. In addition, I was honored to serve as president of the New York Board of the National Music Foundation, chaired nationally by Dick Clark.

I also launched a radio syndication company, which produced and distributed four weekly shows to over seventy-five radio stations around the country.

And now we get to the reason for this book — which will be told, as much as possible, in the artists' own words.

During the interviews, besides discussing the obvious — the music, the stories behind it, the motivation — I dug deeply into the nitty-gritty of the artists' lives. And what stories they had to tell! As I listened to the details of the good, the bad and the ugly, I was struck by the universality of many of their experiences. They had been through what many of us have undergone ourselves.

We all try our best. We all face success and failure, and hopefully, in the end, we pull ourselves up by our bootstraps and go on, sometimes to greater success than we could have imagined. I realized the superstars we idolized were merely men and women trying to live their lives and build careers just like everyone else.

There was the glitz! The excitement! The adulation! The money! I want to be any one of them!! Granted, their lives may have been more glamorous, financially rewarding (in some cases) and dazzling than ours, but underneath we all share a common trait: humanity. As Chuck Negron of Three Dog Night so eloquently pointed out, "There are common bonds in this world for all people. If you can look for the similarities instead of the differences, your life will be a little easier."

I am so grateful for the Decades channels on Sirius XM radio and other means of downloading and streaming, so I can keep accessing songs from the '50s, '60s and '70s, which are my particular favorite eras. PBS stations keep the music alive, primarily through the devoted efforts of TJ Lubinsky. Reunion concerts are constantly still filling venues around the country. Performers have repeatedly told me how parents are bringing their children and grandchildren to the concerts and how beloved the music has become to younger generations, something I've seen for myself.

I'm so happy to be able to share some important insights I gathered from these artists while I was sitting behind the mic. Mainly, it takes grit, great determination, herculean effort, and stamina just to live our lives.

We are all just human beings.

But the greatest takeaway of all? Be careful what you wish for!!

CHAPTER 1
New York

It certainly didn't take television shows to acknowledge that America's got talent…tons of it oozing out of every pore of our country from the smallest dots on the map to the largest cities across our land. Since the first settlers hit Jamestown, voices have risen from cotton fields, bayous, choir lofts, street corners, local hang-outs, the canyons of Tin Pan Alley, and stadiums full of fans.

In the 1940s and '50s, American music was changing drastically. With this evolution, the tempos and rhythms of the lives of white American adults were irrevocably altered. Up to this point, there had been gospel, blues, Western swing, big bands, and regional sounds…but now, many parents felt this new stuff their kids were listening to was exposing them to the devil. They'd go straight to hell for swooning over the gyrating hips of Elvis Presley. "Race music" from black performers often had lyrics that were too racy to be within their kids' earshot. Teen idols were singing their hearts out to their babysitters, neighbors, and girlfriends on whom they had hopeless, pre-pubescent crushes. Holy crap! What had this world come to?

The truth is it had come to a cataclysmic juncture. Innocence, purity, and subtlety had met their match in the hard-driving, sexually arousing, vital, energetic lyrics and beat. The new sound was dubbed "rock and roll" by Cleveland disc jockey Alan Freed, and it was stirring the souls and loins of America's pre-teen and teenage population. The post-World War II "Baby Boom" generation was starting to sit up and take notice, responding to their social environment, trying to figure out how to interpret the mixed signals it was receiving. In a *Rolling Stone* Magazine article, musicologist Robert Palmer (not to be confused with the late artist who had a huge hit with "Addicted to Love") pointed out that Memphis recording pioneer Sam Phillips recognized that the music of the mid-to late '50s was the first popular music aimed directly at the nation's teenagers, thus allowing "marginal" America - poor white sharecroppers, black ghetto youth, and storefront record label operations - the opportunity to express themselves freely. They were no longer limited to providing entertainment exclusively for specialized audiences.

Out of the volcanic ashes from this eruption rose, phoenix-like, a new era of performers and sounds. Some were flash-in-the-pans... others were to become superstars whose music is indelibly woven into the tapestries of our lives.

These are the tales of eight of them whose journeys began in hometowns that reached from coast to coast, west to east: the hills and flats of Los Angeles... Detroit, the Midwestern city that got America rolling down the road...and the burgeoning metropolises of Atlanta and New York City.

*****

It was in the borough of Brooklyn, specifically the Brighton Beach section, where **Neil Sedaka** began his life. In the 1940s, the area was a haven for lower-to-middle class Jewish families, most of them emigrés from the Soviet Union, who spoke Russian and Yiddish in their homes and to each other. During the summer months, the population of the neighborhood would swell considerably, as thousands of *schvitzing* New Yorkers took the BMT subway to the very last stop, looking forward to splashing in the Atlantic surf to cool off. Nearby the older yentas sat in their chairs people-watching and gossiping. It was homogeneous, to say the least. There were some wise-ass local tough guys among the residents, but Neil was definitely not among them. Rather, he was a self-professed wuss whose only companions were his mom Eleanor, his sister Ronnie, his aunts, and his music. He had no friends. Mrs. Sedaka did everything for him, including walking him to school every day (since there were streets that had to be crossed!) and feeding him every meal for the first seven years of his life.

Despite attempts to teach himself how to walk and carry his books like his more masculine schoolmates (as "masculine" as one could be at that age), by the time Neil was in the first grade, he was known to all as the school sissy. His self-image and future outlook were bleak.

Thank heaven for Mrs. Glantz, a second-grade teacher who led the class choir. She was the first one to recognize Neil's musical aptitude. Thrilled at the possibility that her son might be a budding prodigy, Mrs. Sedaka took a job in order to buy her son a second-hand piano, on which he took lessons and practiced constantly. Eventually, Neil's piano teacher felt it was time for his pupil to move on, and suggested he audition for the prestigious Julliard Prep Division for Children - internationally renowned as the educational vehicle for many of the most celebrated musicians in the world. By the age of nine, he had been awarded a scholarship and had begun his training, further fueling his intent to become a concert pianist.

But the popular music of the day had started heading in another direction, and the piano prodigy was intrigued. By the time he was thirteen, Neil and his apartment building neighbor, Howie Greenfield, tried their hand at writing. Their collaboration began after Mrs. Greenfield heard Neil perform and insisted that he meet her son, "the poet." Neil had no idea how to write, and his sixteen-year-old new pal didn't think much of the new rock and roll sound their classmates were dancing to; he considered it a fad. However, they kept meeting and together managed to crank out "My Life's Devotion," which was awful. That notwithstanding, Sedaka loved the experience - and soon not only were the duo knocking out a song a day, but the pop beat grabbed such a hold of Neil that he began to neglect his classical studies.

He had discovered rock and roll! And thank God he did, because that was what catapulted him to hero status among his peers. Another tune he and Howie had written, "Mr. Moon," created pandemonium among his schoolmates every time it was played. From then on, the shy, nerdy kid with the dominating mother was in demand at parties and other social events. Everyone who had sneered at, derided, or otherwise humiliated Neil in the past was now clamoring to be his friend.

In 1955, he formed a Lincoln High School group called the Linc-Tones (later to morph into the Tokens), consisting of Eddie Rabkin,

The Linc-Tones (l. to r.)
Hank Medress, Cynthia Zolotin, Neil Sedaka, and
Eddie Rabkin [Photo credit: James Kriegsmann/
Michael Ochs Archives/Getty Images]

Cynthia Zolotin, and Hank Medress. Jay Siegel replaced Rabkin and has noted that while other groups were performing covers of other writers, their repertoire consisted of songs written by Neil and Howie. Sedaka considered the group an extension of his creative writing - and a great way to make money, since they performed at school dances, and other events. The group managed to get signed to a small independent label, Melba Records, which had placed two major hits on the charts by then: "Alone" by the Sheppard Sisters, and the Willows' "Church Bells May Ring." By the way…that was young master Sedaka playing the chimes at the beginning of that 1956 doo-wop classic.

That same year, when Neil was a senior at Lincoln, he won a city-wide piano competition and was named best in New York by world-renown pianist Arthur Rubenstein. The reward was an appearance on the city's classical radio station, WQXR. That fall, he enrolled at the prestigious Julliard School of Music.

The Tokens recorded "I Love My Baby" which made a brief noise in the New York metropolitan area. Then it fizzled. Kaput. Dead. Neil and his brother-in-law co-wrote "Never Again" which became an R&B hit for Sedaka's idol, Dinah Washington, and also made deejay Peter Tripp's Top 40 list on WMGM. As Neil told me on Kool 96:

> *I discovered I could write songs at thirteen and Howard Greenfield and I started writing very early, and the career took a turn and I started writing for people on Atlantic Records, when I was a teenager: Dinah Washington, Lavern Baker, and Clyde McPhatter.*

Before his sixteenth birthday, Neil had two Top 40 hits to his credit and New Yorkers were beginning to take notice of him.

The roll he was on hit a snag, according to Sadaka, because deejay Alan Freed, whose radio shows were wildly popular in the tri-state area, mistakenly played the "B" side of the Tokens release, "While I Dream," on which Sedaka sang lead. Jealousy allegedly then reared its ugly head. Neil's crush on Cynthia Zolotin caused him to give her numerous leads on their songs, which another group member reportedly resented. After they made an appearance on Dick Clark's TV show *American Bandstand,* Neil departed from the group. The Tokens then reorganized with Jay, Hank, Mitch Margo and his brother Phil. This is the lineup that recorded the #1 hit heard 'round the world, "The Lion Sleeps Tonight" in 1961.

A great deal of the pop music heard on AM radio (the FM band was virtually non-existent at the time) and *American Bandstand* originated and was published in New York City in an area known as "Tin Pan Alley". The places that spawned the hits the adolescent writers were getting published were the stately art deco Brill Building at 1619 Broadway and another at 1650 Broadway. Regardless of where they were actually written, the collective output became known as the Brill Building sound.

> *We were called the Brill Building School of Music: Carole King, Neil Diamond, Paul Simon...and, ah, it was kind of a phenomenon, because Brooklyn produced quite a few very talented people. I went to school with Mort Schuman and of course Neil Diamond and Barry Manilow were in that area too.*

It was in 1650 Broadway that Howie and Neil auditioned their new song, "Stupid Cupid" for the president of Hill and Range. He passed on it. But as they were leaving, they met songwriters Doc Pomus and Mort Schuman, who put the teenagers on to a new publishing house, Aldon Music, whose name derived from its two owners, Al Nevins and Don Kirshner. Not only did they sign the duo to an exclusive songwriting contract, but also signed Neil to a manager-artist deal.

Pivotal to their personal and professional lives was a meeting Kirshner had arranged for them with a hot new teenage star named Connie Francis. She had already been on the first *Dick Clark's Saturday Night Show* lip-synching her huge hit "Who's Sorry Now." She didn't particularly like any of Neil and Howie's ballads but loved their up-tempo "Stupid Cupid" on which Neil played the piano. It made the Billboard Best Seller and Hot 100 charts, and made quite a bit of money for the singer-songwriters. Suddenly it was respectable to be a songwriter! While basking in the glory of the MGM hit, Neil admits RCA Victor, the home of Elvis Presley was really the label he wanted to record for. In 1958, RCA's Steve Sholes signed him after hearing a demo of a song Neil had originally intended for another group.

> *I wrote a song for Little Anthony and the Imperials called "The Diary." It was supposed to be the follow-up to "Tears on My Pillow," and they recorded it, but put it in the can as we say, and that did become my very first hit on RCA.*

Subsequently, he had "Stupid Cupid" and "Frankie" under his belt as well as a 1959 Grammy nomination for "The Diary." Between 1958 and 1962, Neil racked up nine Billboard Top-20 hits including "Oh! Carol," "Stairway to Heaven," "Calendar Girl," and "Happy Birthday, Sweet Sixteen". His "Breaking Up Is Hard to Do" was also nominated for the 1962 Grammy Award for Best Rock and Roll Recording. (A newly-recorded version was also nominated for the 1976 Song Of The Year.) After a break from recording in the United States, he had #1 hits with "Laughter In The Rain" and "Bad Blood," the latter recorded with Elton John. He was further honored when "Love Will Keep Us Together," sung by the Captain & Tennille, was tapped as the

1975 Record of the Year and was nominated for Song of the Year as well. He would continue to chart songs for decades after.

As Neil said to me on Kool 96:

> *You know, I was also a very disciplined serious musician and I knew that I wanted to travel the world as a singer-songwriter. I used to watch Dick Clark's American Bandstand as a teenager and I dreamed of being on there myself singing my own records. I was a very positive thinker. As a matter of fact, I used to buy all these 45s and take a pen and cross out, on the label, the name of the singer and put my name down to see how it looked in print. I really didn't project the scope of it.*

Now that's an understatement!!

Now in his sixth decade in show business, Neil's songs have been sung by the widest and most diverse array of talent imaginable, including among others, ABBA, the Carpenters, Nick Carter, Elvis Presley, Teresa Brewer, Cher, Petula Clark, Neil Diamond, Bobby Darin, Patsy Cline, Queen, Lesley Gore, Crystal Gale, Jan & Dean, Suzannah McCorkle, Wilson Picket, Sha Na Na… and the three Jones boys: Davy, Jack, and Tom. He was honored with the Sammy Kahn Lifetime Achievement Award, inducted into the Songwriters Hall of Fame, and earned a star on the Hollywood Walk of Fame. In 2004, he was a guest judge on *"American Idol"* (runner-up Clay Aiken sang his song "Solitaire", propelling Neil to #4 on the Hot 100 Singles chart) and has even parodied his own songs in the childrens' album, *Waking up Is Hard to Do*. Sedaka was honored in

1997 with a tribute at New York's Lincoln Center, and on October 12, 2012, he released his first acoustic album, which concludes with his first piano concerto, "Manhattan Intermezzo," recorded with the Philharmonic Orchestra of London. To this day, Neil Sedaka continues to write, produce, and perform all over the world. His latest collection is *I Do It for Applause,* containing a dozen new songs. In 2019, Moravian College in Bethlehem, Pennsylvania honored Neil with a Doctor of Music degree.

Not too shabby for a little Jewish wuss from Brooklyn!

*****

Her name and face might not have been a household word or image, but the list of songs, accomplishments, and honors of singer-song/jingle writer and producer **Ellie Greenwich** is nearly as long as Neil Sedaka's.

Born in Brooklyn and raised on Long Island, Eleanor Louise Greenwich also began her road to success as a teenager. She says she knew she'd be doing something in music from the day she was born, always having loved music in any form, innately knowing that she had to do it.

> *Always. If I wasn't, seriously, if I wasn't dancing to it, I was doing something.*

As she told me in our interview on Kool 96:

> *I was very fortunate; I knew somebody, who knew somebody, who knew somebody and I think if I ever renamed one of my companies, it would be Fluke Productions.*

Cadence Record Company president Archie Bleyer, whose roster included the Everly Brothers and the Chordettes, gave Ellie some of the best advice of her life. He suggested she finish her education while she could because the music business would always be there. Wisely, she listened.

First attending Queens College, Ellie transferred to Hofstra College, earning her B.A. in English and making it into *Who's Who in American Colleges*. She next found herself a teaching job...for less than a month.

> *What happened was because I switched my major, I graduated mid-term instead of June. It was February. So when I went to apply for a job they put me in with high school seniors and they wanted to get out of school. So I walk in and I'm goin' "hello" and they're going "Hey, hi ya." So I had very little control over the classes that I had. It was fun."*

If you liked it so much, why did you leave?

> *'Cause the principal said, 'This is silly. I mean, you're not controlling these kids." I said, "No, I'm not. I understand." And he goes, "I know that you're seriously into music. Why don't you go try that?" Seriously, 'cause he knew I was torn between being a teacher and being at least what I studied and what my mother and father spent some money on sending me to school. And I said, "Oh, okay," and that was it.*

I suggested to her that such a leap of faith took real guts. She agreed, noting she had very supportive parents and since music was in her blood, everyone knew that eventually, she'd have to give it a try. She figured sooner was better than later. And through that "fluke" she referred to, she soon wound up in one of the most sacred edifices in New York, the Brill Building. Occupants of the small offices were predominantly those who were making things happen in the world of popular music, including agents, promoters, and approximately ninety music publishers.

Her memories, as she described them to me on Kool 96, were very vivid. She recalled the thrill of just walking into the building because even the lobby was so alive and exciting. There was the Turf restaurant on the left and Jack Dempsey's on the right, where from mid-morning on, there were people making deals. Successful artists and wannabes were milling around…

> …*singing in the lobby, whatever; you'd get in the elevator and you'd go up through the floors and you'd be hearing music playing on all the floors.*

On each floor were doors upon doors of tiny offices belonging to publishers, with hopeful songwriters making their way down from the top floor, which housed Elvis' publishers Hill and Range. If you were one of the lucky ones, you'd sell your tune for about $25-$35 dollars, which would maybe amount to carfare and lunch.

Through somebody who knew somebody, Ellie wound up in Jerry Leiber and Mike Stoller's Trio Music/Leiber-Stoller Productions office. At the time she had no idea who they were.

I remember that day I was waiting for this guy John Gluck, Jr. who was the gentleman that somebody who knew somebody who knew somebody in my family told me to meet at the Brill Building in this room. And I sat in this little cubbyhole with my sorority jacket on from school, and I was playing piano and singing. And Jerry Leiber came in and said, "Oh, Carole," and I was so scared and I introduced myself. He was evidently expecting Carole King up there that day. And that was the beginning of my life.

Ellie started working there on a first-refusal basis. She told me she was dating Jeff Barry at the time and everything was sort of coming together for her.

I think the only chance I took was saying "yes" to whatever might have come my way. I would knock on the door, and it really opened!

When someone said to come on in and let them hear her songs, she felt it was the most incredible thing that could happen, since all she wanted to do was her thing.

Let me write my song, and if you like it, well, what can I pay you for liking it? It really was sort of like that.

And so began a professional life that became bigger than anyone could have imagined, including Ellie. She had a keen sense of the teen experience of the time and interpreted it as few others could. The list of songs that she wrote, co-wrote, produced, arranged, and sang on, would take pages to cover. In addition, she worked with Phil Spector and was responsible for a number of hits during the girl group era, including the Crystals' "Chapel of Love" and "Leader of the Pack," by the Shangri-Las. Ellie later performed the tune herself during a semi-autobiographical show that ran on Broadway, *Leader Of The Pack.* The show was nominated for a Tony Award and a Grammy for the cast album, and won the New York Music Award for Best Broadway Musical.

From early in her career, Ellie held the title of "Demo Queen" for all the singing she did on them. She also sang on jingles, often writing them as well, touting such products as Cheerios, Ford, and Clairol; she was nominated for Clio Awards for her "Ooo- La -La Sasson" jeans and Prince Albert Tobacco spots, and even won the award for a Levi's "Be My Baby" commercial.

One of her collaborators during her stellar career was Tony Powers, with whom she charted with a hit by the Exciters ("He's Got The Power"), as well as smashes credited to Darlene Love "((Today I Met) The Boy I'm Gonna Marry") and Bob B. Soxx And The Blue Jeans ("Why Do Lovers Break Each Other's Heart?"). Both were also co-written and produced by Phil Spector. Ellie also had great success working with Doc Pomus, Shadow Morton, Bob Crewe, and other superstars of the music business.

In 1962, Ellie and Jeff Barry married and within a year they scored a pair of blockbuster hits for the Ronettes: "Baby, I Love You" and "Be My Baby", both of which personified Phil Spector's signature "Wall of Sound." He had co-written and produced both. Other collaborations among the three included "Then He Kissed Me" by the Crystals which was a charted hit in 1963, and a song which Darlene

Ellie Greenwich and Jeff Barry in the studio, 1964
[Photo credit: Michael Ochs Archives/Getty Images]

Love still sings today during the Yule season, "Christmas (Baby Please Come Home)."

Nineteen sixty-three was a pivital year for the duo. Along with Ellie's sister Laura, they called themselves The Raindops and made the Top-20 on the Billboard Hot 100 chart with "The Kind of Boy You Can't Forget." The following year, their song "Do Wah Diddy Diddy," released by Manfred Mann, rose to #1. Together they penned and recorded "Hanky Panky," but it didn't become a success until Tommy James and the Shondells rode it to the top of the U.S. charts in 1966.

Sadly the Greenwich-Barry marriage had ended the year before.

In 1991, Ellie and Jeff were inducted into the Songwriters Hall of Fame. Seven years later, Ellie was a recipient of the Touchstone Award by Women in Music, and in 2010 Ellie and Jeff were inducted into the Rock & Roll Hall of Fame by Carole King in the non-performer category.

Ellie's music has been recorded by a wide spectrum of artists – from the Beach Boys, the Young Rascals, Elvis Presley, Ike & Tina Turner, and Lesley Gore to Blondie, Rick Nelson, Eddie Money, and Dusty Springfield. In 1997, she had a #1 record on both the Pop and Dance charts in England and Australia with "Sunshine After the Rain." Six years later her "River Deep-Mountain High" came in at #9 on a list of the 100 Greatest Songs Ever as voted by the Australian press. Recorded originally by Ike & Tina Turner, and then Deep Purple, it peaked at #14 in 1971 after being recorded by the Supremes and Four Tops.

Here's a major detail about Ellie you may not have known: it was she who discovered and talked Jeff into meeting Neil Diamond! The rest, as they say…..

Ellie was working on a book and developing other projects when on August 26, 2009, she succumbed to a heart attack while in a New York hospital being treated for pneumonia. She was sixty-eight years young. In her memory, Hofstra University has dedicated a "Garden of Ellie," in which there's a statue of her adjacent to the school's music school.

Full disclosure: she had become a dear personal friend through the years and just like the rest of the music industry, I miss her dearly.

*****

(l. to r.) Neil Diamond, Ellie Greenwich, Bert Burns, Jeff Barry
[Photo credit: PoPsie Randolph/Michael Ochs Archives/Getty Images]

Another borough of New York City, the Bronx, was home to **Chuck Negron** and his twin sister, Nancy. Their dad, Charles, had enlisted in the U.S. Navy before his children had turned two, returning in 1945 with veterans' benefits but little ambition to be anything but a singer. Mom Betty, twenty-two years old with two young kids, worked for a while in Bloomingdale's photo studio after dropping the twins off at a city-sponsored nursery school. Finally, his parents split, and his mother had to put young Charlie and Nancy in an orphanage. It was a devastating, morale-breaking nightmare.

Finally, by the sixth grade, the twins were back home again, but not without a great toll having been taken, especially on Charlie. He was emotionally scarred, with extremely poor self-esteem. Luckily, two things turned his life around.

> *When I would wander the streets as a young man, you know I would go and see the guys playin' ball and one day they invited me in. And I had a gift for it. It was the most wonderful feeling, having people go, I mean people older than me, 'cause I had no male figures, going "Hey, man, you're good." I made the Taft [High School] varsity team my first year. By the time I was a senior, I was an All-City selection from the Bronx with several college scholarship offers in my pocket. Basketball had become my identity. It gave me freedom and joy and I wasn't a scared stupid loser anymore. Basketball was the first thing I ever did well. And it defined me and it gave me the opportunity to realize no matter how much pain you carry along with you, what fear, if you have something you do well and find it, go for it, no matter what it is. And it saved my life and actually gave me the opportunity to sing because I was too shy. I never would never have sung. If I didn't already realize that there was one thing I did well, maybe I could do this well too.*
>
> *I realized that at the same time something else was developing that one day would catapult me beyond my wildest dreams.*

These guys played basketball and then they would sing. You know, some of them, along with all the other guys, would be out there hangin', you know, drinkin' and smoking pot and whatever, and singin' harmony. [My friend the late] *Bobby Pittari was really into music and you know he turned me on to* [New York deejays] *Symphony Sid and Jocko, who was playin' black music. I mean real black music, and then Alan Freed, was in the scene playin' you know, doo-wop and black music, so I knew these songs. So when I go, "Oh, man, I know that one," they'd go, "Where'd you hear that?" because, you know, it wasn't in the white mainstream. So they'd invite me to sing and I'd start singing, and the same thing with the basketball happened with the singing.*

Charlie's friends were in shock that this outstanding jock also had quite a voice. He was as amazed as his cohorts and lapped up the attention. Somewhere along the way, he had become "Chuck", and along with his buddies, realized he had something special going for him. Once again, he was cool.

Doo-wop was wonderful. We sang all the songs on the corner and, oh, God, it was a ball...in the subway, downtown, in Harlem...We played everywhere. Then Bob Pittari, who really wanted to be an entertainer, formed a group and he encouraged me. We started singing and formed a quintet that was called the Rondells. So then a year from 1957 to 1958, we made a record with good writers: Ricardo Weeks, who wrote "I Wonder Why" for Dion and the Belmonts, and some black songs you wouldn't know from doo-wop groups, and, uh, man, the record "Bells Of My Heart" landed us a gig at the Apollo.

It was a very scary thing. The woman before us was really not liked and they started yelling at her, then the microphone started disappearing into the floor, then a clown with a hook came and took her off the stage. We were about ready to leave at this point.

Then they pushed us, and said, "You're on," and we went out there, and I have to say something, that the audience, which was totally black, didn't think all these kids in their green sweaters were very cute. And it was silent. But the wonderful thing about music was that by the second verse, they were cheering us on. And I learned a lesson that day, and I've said it many times...that music and things and sports transcend all color barriers and all differences. And I was accepted, and it really was a powerful message to me that there are common bonds in this world for all people. If you can look for the similarities instead of the differences your life will be a little easier. And it was a great lesson as a young kid.

Despite making a number of demos for record companies and writers, the Rondells began getting interested in girls and other things, and the group died a slow but painless death - just in time for Chuck to explore the halls of higher education. He opted for Hancock, a two-year college in southern California, where he could be near his father and stepmother. The school gave him a full scholorship and helped get him a job with the local parks department, working with kids.

Eventually, though, he dropped out. He felt the time he had spent there had given him all he asked for: success in sports, singing, friendships, and newly-found self-confidence, which bolstered his self-esteem. Most importantly, it gave him a great deal of time to bond with the father he sorely missed following his parents' divorce.

He played basketball, naturally, but suffered a lot of injuries. Despite that, he still continued vocalizing. Without his knowledge, the people Chuck worked with at Columbia Records planned to groom him as a crooner, the next Johnnie Mathis, despite his extremely eclectic sound. By the mid-1960s, America had been swept away by the British Invasion. Because the music execs at the label were failing to read the trends correctly, Chuck's career with them was dead. So back he went for the summer to his old Bronx neighborhood, which, sadly, was now riddled with drugs. He then returned to Los Angeles where he was introduced to Danny Hutton at a party for Donovan. That night turned out to be quite a turning point for the young singer…it was here he became irrevocably hooked into the drug scene and sexual revolution.

> *I met Danny at a party, very casually. He was a nice guy; you know I mean he was a really "up" guy and had a record that was being played around town, so I knew him. And anyway, I went home with a girl that night, and I was living in my car. And she said, "No, I'm living with a friend, come stay with me." One thing led to another, her asking me what I did. I went to my car and got my records and from the*

other room this guy said, "Hey, man you really can sing, but those records are outdated." He was one of the guys Danny Hutton worked with as a producer. So Danny and I became very good friends; we hung around together; we had a lot of fun. I enjoyed being with him. And I went off one summer and did a tour with [deejay] *Dick Biondi for the Job Corps. You know, it was a freebie, but I needed to get my chops together because I was working in the May Company as manager of the cosmetics department and doing gigs at night. So anyway when I came back my voice was in great shape.*

Danny called me and said, "Hey, I got this guy over here, Cory Wells, and have an idea of putting something together. Why don't you come over?" I went over, and the second we sang, it was magic. I mean, what happened when the three of us sang was unbelievable. And they asked me to join the band and of course I said yes, 'cause I knew who Cory was. I'd never met him but I knew who he was because of his success at the Whisky [A Go Go], *right around the time when Johnny Rivers was there...when the Whiskey was the hottest place. He had been in a movie; he was playing all the parties for Elizabeth Taylor; his band was the Enemies, because that's what happened when you played in L.A. You became part of the whole scene. So I knew who he was and boom, there I am. I'm in the band and we start recording.*

Danny's idea for the group was unique and wound up pretty much defining its sound: all three members were going to be singing lead, depending on which song seemed to fit which individual best.

> *I think it moved into another thing because Danny and Cory wrote. I didn't write that much, so I started bringing in the material which was different from what they were doing.*

Chuck literally went on a mission to seek out new writers whose material he could adopt and perform.

> *So we started with the management, hittin' all the writers and I found out about Barry Mann and Cynthia Weill, Leiber and Stoller, Goffin and King, Bacharach and David, the people that were the architects of rock and roll.*

And where did they go to find them? Surprise, surprise… to the Brill Building, of course!

> *We were at the Brill Building three days a week, going to hundreds of offices, you know, trying to get them to sign us to get some songs. So when Three Dog Night came together, I said, You know, now I have some muscle, 'cause I couldn't get a song"* [in earlier attempts]. *And I went in and met these guys. That's how I got Harry Nilsson, that's how I got to Paul Williams,* [and] *Laura Nyro. Boom! I was off! In the first album, I think I have about five or six songs that I brought, such as Nilsson's "One."*

That kind of pushed the band. Chuck then proposed "Eli's Coming" penned by his friend Laura Nyro.

> *And it kinda developed by the material that I did my thing, Cory did his thing, and then Danny did his thing. But it was very hard for them not to cross over because in the beginning I had so much success, so it was a very good thing that they kept the faith. You know, my thing changed, and then they started having hits.*

> *We had heard Randy Newman 'cause Van Dyke Parks, one of our producers, had worked with him. We had heard his songs but we didn't know Cory had been doing "Mama Told Me" in his act when he was a solo artist, so he actually brought that tune to us. And then I brought Paul Williams' songs "Out In The Country" and "Old Fashioned Love Song," and Danny found "Black and White." So we all kinda brought tunes.*

And then there was their odd-ball name.

> *There was a magazine called Mankind and there was an article about the aborigines, a specific tribe, a very small tribe in the Outback, and their expression for a very cold night was a "three dog night". That's how they stated it and we put it on our list, and when we told the record company that name, they flipped out... "That's disgusting, we don't like it." And we went 'That's it!'*

(l. to r.) Cory Wells, Chuck Negron, Danny Hutton
[Photo credit: Alan Messer/Shutterstock]

That was the start of the road for the group...a road that would have more bumps, ruts, dead ends and stop signs than anyone could have foreseen. Over a six-year span, 1969 to 1975, they had twenty-one consecutive Top-40 hits, and a dozen straight gold LPs. One single, "Joy to the World" was also a cross-over R&B entry. The song was nominated for a 1971Grammy in the Best Pop Vocal Performance category but lost to Karen and Richard Carpenter's self-titled album. Nine of their songs were Adult Contemporary hits; both "An Old Fashioned Love Song" and "Black & White" scooted to the top pole position.

Then they disbanded.

Chuck's personal and professional journey after that is one of the most agonizing ones to even think about. His rebound and dedication to life today are extraordinary.

CHAPTER 2
Atlanta and Detroit

If you start in New York City and travel approximately 750 miles south, you'll reach the city of Atlanta, Georgia – which is where, on May 28, 1944, **Gladys Knight** made her debut. The third of four children born to Merald Knight and the former Sarah Elizabeth Woods, she joined Brenda (1941), and Merald Jr. a/k/a "Bubba" (1942). Baby David arrived in 1947. Their father was one of the first African-American postal employees in a city where poor black families were striving very hard for their share of the American dream.

As she related her early life to me on KOOL 96:

> *I came from a family of workers, of doers, of dreamers, of all those things of spiritual people. And so I had role models, people that I could emulate…my father was a workaholic…he had three jobs…we had great work ethics.*

Gladys was singing practically from the crib. Her mother immediately recognized her younger daughter's talent, a special gift that enabled her to belt out, rather than just "sing" a song. In her young world, the music was strictly gospel. While others were thunderstruck by what they were hearing, little Gladys couldn't understand what all the fuss was about...all she was doing was singing. What could possibly be so special?

Actually, she was embarrassed by the attention she got as a youngster. She was more interested in playing with friends, having a normal childhood, and indulging in one of her favorite activities: cooking. She loved to experiment with recipes, and many years later, would write her own cookbook.

When Gladys thought back on her younger years, what stood out in her mind was getting dragged away from playing or watching television or whatever else she was involved in, in order to sing. It took a lot of coaxing on her mother's part to drag her away, but she always wound up doing what was asked.

She was not the only family member who could vocalize. After the dinner dishes were cleared, the Knights would sit back down as a family and sing their praises to God. As with most black families in the south at this time, the church played a huge role within Gladys' family. Her parents were both with the Wings Over Jordan and Mount Moriah choirs, while she and Bubba were in the Sunbeam Children's Choir. They eventually formed the Youth For Christ Choir.

Used to performing for an audience of supportive family and friends, Gladys's first solo recital came at the ripe old age of four at a church benefit. She actually got paid for her performance!

Fast forward three years later: Momma Knight truly believed that seven-year-old Gladys had a special talent that needed a wider audience. In direct opposition to her husband's orders, she contacted the powers that be at a national television show, *The Original Amateur Hour* – a precursor to talent-seeking shows like *American Idol*. It first aired on radio in 1934 with Major Edward Bowes as host, and in 1948, after Bowes' passing, his talent scout Ted Mack brought it to television. It ended up being one of the few programs to run on all four commercial networks of the era and was consistently one of the highest-rated shows on the air. More than forty years later, it was resurrected as *The New Original Amateur* Hour on The Family Channel, with Willard Scott as host. From its start on New York City's WHN radio through its last first-run television season in 1970, it's estimated that more than one million aspiring stars were among those who auditioned.

After she was accepted as a contestant, the show paid for Gladys, her mother, and her brother Bubba to come to New York City to audition. The hustle and bustle, the traffic, and brusqueness of the big city were quite a culture shock. When they got to the theater, it was obvious to all that this little southern girl was younger, shorter, and certainly darker than the other hopefuls. Neither daunted nor nervous, Gladys sang what had become an old standby for her, "Braham's Lullaby". She knocked it out of the ballpark and was chosen to compete on the next show. Since this would be days later, the Knights returned to Atlanta - while the ballot box got stuffed with as many votes as the friends and family could generate. Keep in mind, there were no 800 numbers to call or text votes to tilt the outcome; in those days, votes for favorites were sent via the old-fashioned way: snail mail.

After winning the first round and two subsequent ones, Gladys turned eight, lost her first tooth…and was named the National Radio Champion of 1952. Not surprisingly, as a third-grader, she had no clue about what national exposure and $2,000 in prize money meant.

After her victory, her mother turned down the chance for Gladys to become the star of her own television show but did accept an invite for her to be the guest of honor at a performance in Atlanta starring Nat King Cole, Sarah Vaughn, and Billy Eckstein.

When she finally returned to grade school, except for an occasional performance, Gladys was able to relax and enjoy being a kid once more.

In 1952 Bubba turned ten. At the party celebrating that milestone, a record player allegedly malfunctioned, so the Knight clan and cousins William and Eleanor Guest started singing together – and a group was born. The one condition was that the kids would stay in the church choir.

They worked hard at getting their sound together, and since a cousin, James "Pip" Woods had some pull in the local club scene, Mrs. Knight roped him into managing the group. They began rehearsing at his house, working on both their vocalizing and choreography, and their first engagement took place at a ladies' auxiliary club tea at the YMCA. It was a start. After that came fish fries, local frat parties, and family reunions. It wasn't until several months later, after Pip entered them in a talent show at the El Morocco Lounge in Atlanta, that the ensemble chose a name. They definitely didn't want anything similar to ones that were popular at the time like birds (*e.g.*, the Orioles) or cars (*e.g.,* the Cadillacs), so…surprise…they became the Pips. What a stretch!

After three weeks of competition, the group won the grand prize: two weeks at the Royal Peacock, a legendary club in town where many of the greatest rhythm and blues and rock and roll acts started out. More excited about the fun and exposure than the ten bucks a night they made for two shows, the Pips not only aced the two-week tryout, but they became the house group! Mind you, under ordinary circumstances, the youngsters would never have made it past the front door. Gladys was all of nine years old at the time. But she was hardly an inexperienced kid, considering all she'd accomplished by then – even if she was still relegated to their manager's car in the parking lot to do her homework.

The Royal Peacock gig did the trick. In the following years, she and the Pips appeared in their hometown a great deal. Their act also took them on the Chitlin' Circuit, a string of venues that wove through the landscape of the south and east, featuring black acts performing for black audiences. Besides the more well-known places, like the Apollo Theater and Cotton Club in New York, and the Howard Theater in Washington, D.C., they also booked gigs at joints that were no more than roadhouses and honky-tonks where drag queens and hard-core performers considered the youngsters part of their family.

The road trips may have been occasionally gritty, but the Pips closely watched over Gladys protecting her as much as they could from the seedier side of the business. She told me:

> *You know they really, really took good care of me, almost to the point where they gave me, you know, this thing where I thought it was something wrong with me cause the guys never approached me...they never came near me!*

By the time Gladys was eleven, she and the Pips had reached the point where they were on the verge of becoming a national act, and the family thought it was important to find a music mentor/vocal coach for her. Enter Maurice King, the musical director at the Flame Show Bar and Fox Theaters in Detroit, who also worked with such future Motown superstars such as the Supremes and Temptations.

Year after year, King worked with the group, nudging them toward harmonic and presentation perfection. Looking to promote his pro-tégés, "Pops" booked them for local gigs, one of which included singing live radio jingles for Parker House Sausages in exchange for breakfast in a Detroit restaurant! Quid pro quo, I guess. The broadcasts led to recording a song, "Whistle My Love." It bombed.

The rigors of being on the road so much took its toll on sister Brenda Knight and cousin Eleanor Guest, who decided enough was enough. Both left the group to finish school and start families. Cousins Edward Patten and Langston George then stepped up and rounded out the quintet in 1959. Langston left in 1962, and the group remained a quartet.

When school was out, they would spend their summers back on the road. Gladys was twelve when they joined the Supersonic Attractions tour, sharing the bill with two supernovas of the era, Jackie Wilson and Sam Cooke. Of course, she was still under the watchful eye of the guys in the group.

There was a problem, though. Gladys began feeling less and less like she needed as much protection as she was getting. Her fame was growing and her reputation as a "good girl" was intact. Yet she still longed to go to college to major in home economics. By now,

Gladys Knight and the Pips
[Photo credit: Everett Collection/ Shutterstock]

everything she had witnessed on the wilder side of the business - the pills, the drinking, the drugs, and parties - didn't attract or interest her in the least. She wanted was to be in the kitchen talking recipes.

With her father's withdrawal from the household due to personal issues, all of the Knight children took on additional part-time jobs to give their mother some financial relief. It was a stressful time for Gladys who only wanted to be a normal teenager. Singing and high school were her salvation during this time. She busied herself with a load of activities at Archer High, like the cheerleading squads, choir, and yearbook staff. She also had a large circle of friends who were high achievers and goal setters, which gave her the joy and security of being part of the "in" crowd.

The icing on the cake was when the school's band director, Lloyd Terry, introduced Gladys to the reigning royalties of jazz: Ella Fitzgerald, Sarah Vaughn, Oscar Peterson, and others. Terry, who had also filled the emotional gap after Mr. Knight left the family, taught her how to sing jazz and invited her to join his own jazz band, which included weekend gigs all over the Southeast.

Thirteen-year-old Gladys's talent flourished and the band became known as the best in the city. Imagine the thrill of working with Cannonball Adderley, Jimmy Smith, Jimmy McGriff and other greats...let alone opening for Aretha Franklin! But the demands and responsibilities had become burdensome: she didn't want to re-hearse every Wednesday night or perform with the Pips every time a gig came up. She had also started rebelling about singing all three nights of every weekend with the jazz band. All she wanted to do was hang out with her friends. It got to the point where she actually prayed for God to take away her talent!

While in high school, Gladys started seeing Jimmy Newman, a friend of her brother's, three years older than her. He also played in Mr. Terry's jazz band. Having known each other since elementary school the two became close, despite Jimmy's having fathered a son by another girl in school. Since they had shared a love of music, Gladys missed him a lot when he went off to college away from home, and was thrilled when he transferred to Clark University in Atlanta after just one semester. But the joy of music that was such a comfort for Gladys apparently was not shared to the same degree by Jimmy by the time he returned. What comforted him now was marijuana. It wasn't that Gladys and Bubba didn't know anything about it; they were certainly used to its smell and effects from the tour buses. Gladys just didn't want the man she had her heart set on becoming a pothead.

Meanwhile the Pips were counting the days till their lead singer would finish school and be able to tour full-time; however, the six-teen-year-old had other plans. With thoughts of a little house and white picket fence trumping those of gold records and Grammys, she planned to marry Jimmy right after college.

After their gig one evening at the Builder's Club, a popular dance place, the group was asked to hang around because the owner, Fats Hunter, had just bought some new recording equipment he wanted to try out. Obligingly, Gladys and the Pips laid down a new Johnny Otis tune called "Every Beat of My Heart." Soon she began getting compliments on the recording from schoolmates who heard it on the radio, and realized that Hunter had not only stolen the song, but he'd sold the master to Vee-Jay Records, a major label in Chicago.

This was hardly the first time performers had been ripped off; un-scrupulous managers and promoters had been honing the skill for years…for example, claiming there was no gate to split with the talent, despite the obvious fact that the house had been packed. It was the first time, however, that Gladys and the Pips experienced it firsthand.

Because of the heavy promotion Vee-Jay put behind the record, it eventually topped Billboard's R&B chart and went to #6 on the Hot 100. It's no surprise that the group, whose hit was now piling up money for the record label, never saw a dime of it. But there was a plus-side to the injustice: their name was now out there to a huge audience which included Zenas "Daddy" Sears, a very powerful southern disc jockey. Sears was a white man who was a huge supporter of so-called "race" music and had provided a big boost to the careers of Little Richard, Ray Charles and Jerry "The Iceman" Butler, among others. Simultaneously, there were other deejays around the country doing the same, such as Jocko Henderson in New York, Alan Freed out in Cleveland and later in New York, and one of the first early female radio voices, Zilla Mays in Atlanta.

Although no one realized it at the time, their course was set. The group met in New York with Bobby Robinson, the head of Fury Records, and went home with a contract in hand. Literally, right after Gladys' graduation from high school, they were back north to cut a new version of "Every Beat of my Heart". To distinguish the Fury release from the "stolen" earlier one credited to "Pips," the name of the group was changed to "Gladys Knight and the Pips." By 1961 they made music history: both versions of the song made the charts, arriving there on the same day.

Then it happened.

At the age of sixteen, Gladys found out she was pregnant and, with her mom's permission, quietly married Jimmy Newman. So much for the house and picket fence she had dreamed of. Soon, they were back on the road, with Jimmy having been anointed band leader and sax player. Three months into the pregnancy, Gladys suffered a miscarriage. Trouper that she was, she was back performing that night.

Gladys and the Pips went on to rack up twenty-six Pop chart hits between 1961 and 1996, with only one," Midnight Train to Georgia," making it to #1, sitting there for two weeks. But if you check out the R&B chart and you'll get a different picture: fifty-five of their songs appeared during that same period, including "Every Beat of My Heart", "I Heard It Through the Grapevine", "If I Were Your Woman", "Neither One Of Us (Wants To Be The First To Say Goodbye)", "I've Got To Use My Imagination", and "Best Thing That Ever Happened to Me". Gladys also had an additional ten R&B hits as a solo artist, plus appearances in the all-star collaborations "That's What Friends Are For" (with Dionne Warwick, Elton John, and Stevie Wonder) and "Missing You" (with Brandy, Tamia, and Chaka Khan).

All told, Gladys (with and without the Pips) has been nominated for twenty-two Grammy awards, with seven wins – including one as recently as 2005 for her album with the Saints Unified Voices, *One Voice* (Best Gospel Choir or Chorus Album).

As busy as she is, she's also found the time to try her hand in other media. Gladys was in the Tyler Perry film *I Can Do Bad All By Myself,* and among her TV credits are such shows as *30 Rock, Hot In Cleveland, Empire, The Jamie Foxx Show,* and even the original *Baywatch.* She also co-starred with the late Flip Wilson on the CBS-TV show *Charlie & Co.* and has received credit for appearances on programs such as "Las Vegas," and "JAG." Like Neil Sedaka, she has also been a guest judge on *American Idol.* Stretching herself even more, she did two stints on Broadway in 1999 in the smash musical *Smokey Joe's Café.*

Known as the "Empress of Soul," Gladys has been honored numerous times by the music industry. In 1995, she received a star on the Hollywood Walk of Fame and the following year she and her cousins were inducted into the Rock and Roll Hall of Fame. Two years later, she and the Pips received the Lifetime Achievement Award from the Rhythm and Blues Foundation, and in 2005, Gladys was honored with yet another Lifetime Achievement Award, this time from BET (Black Entertainment Television).

"The Empress" was the first African-American entertainer to have a Las Vegas venue named for her (The Gladys Knight Theater in the Tropicana Hotel). In the fall of 2011, she was honored along with Earth, Wind & Fire with the *Soul Train* "Legend Award," and shortly thereafter, she put on her dancing shoes and strutted her stuff on TV's very popular show *Dancing With The Stars.* In 2019 she had the honor of performing the national anthem at Super Bowl LIII back in her hometown of Atlanta.

Gladys has devoted her time and efforts to humanitarian and philanthropic causes: she's a national spokesperson for the American Diabetes Association, (her mother died of complications from the disease), and has worked on behalf of the American Cancer Society, amfAR, and crisis intervention. The NAACP Legal Defense Fund, Congress of Racial Equality (CORE) and B'nai Brith have also publically acknowledged her involvement in their respective causes.

To this day, Gladys Knight remains one of the most talented, endearing, honored performers ever to grace the worldwide entertainment field.

*****

Back in the early sixties if you got in your car in Atlanta, and drove northwest approximately seven hundred miles to Detroit, Michigan, you'd hear the sounds of assembly lines cranking out Ford, General Motors, and Chrysler automobiles. You'd also hear music. Lots of it.

During the seminal decades of the '50s and '60s, the city was inundated with talent, primarily African-American kids from the projects doing everything they could to get their voices heard. You couldn't miss the sounds emanating from everywhere in the Motor City…groups were harmonizing in rec halls and at dances…and radios were always cranked up as loud as possible.

Most of it was showcased in local venues, but later became centralized in a small house at 2638 West Grand Boulevard, dubbed "Hitsville, U.S.A.," where the "Sound Of Young America" was born and nurtured. It would become one of the most historically significant addresses in the history of pop and soul music, overseen by its legendary founder Berry Gordy, a former auto company assembly line worker.

One of the most important groups ever to come out of Motown was the Temptations. Though circumstances would necessitate many personnel changes over the years, **Otis Williams** remains the singular original member who has carried the group's banner into the twenty-first century.

He was born on October 30, 1941, to Hazel Williams and Otis Gooden who never quite got around to marrying each other. Hazel, who was sixteen when her son was born, moved to Detroit, entrusting the child to his grandmother Gooden. In those days, families were often very large, so it wasn't unusual for relatives to help raise some of the children. He would see his mother every so often and his father more, since the elder Otis, or "Sonny One", was the deacon of the church where his grandmothers would take him each week.

As for his love of music:

> *You know I was steeped with going to church every*
> *Sunday and even during the week, and being part*
> *of the choir. On the radio you know you'd hear the*
> *great gospel groups: the Swan Silvertones, Dixie*
> *Hummingbirds, and the Harmonizing Four.*

Otis' home was in an area where he saw and heard various local groups walking to or from their shows. He was especially impressed with a homegrown quintet called the Fresandos and managed to get the group's tenor, David Cryor to join him. Singers were a dime a dozen around town and Otis and David soon picked up a lead singer, a bass singer, and one other guy, forming their own quintet. For various reasons, (sometimes just lack of dedication, which was of great importance to Otis), the members of the group would change. This was pretty common among most of the teenage groups of the era – not only in Detroit, but wherever a cappella, doo-wop, and rock and roll were at a fever pitch.

> *Well, 1956, you know, they were like bringing a lot*
> *of rock and roll shows in and out of Detroit, and*
> *there's a place where we still perform to this very*
> *day called the Fox Theater. I was about fifteen or*
> *sixteen years old and this rock and roll show came*
> *to the Fox. It had Frankie Lyman and the Teenagers,*
> *the Cadillacs, and a whole list of other artists on*
> *there. I was very impressed with the showmanship*
> *and the way the Cadillacs could perform and sing...*
> *their choreography was something to behold, and I*
> *guess about twelve or fifteen years later we would be*

working with Cholly Atkins, who was the choreographer for the Cadillacs at that time..."

The tumult, screaming and the frenzied reaction of thousands of fans convinced Otis that this was what he really wanted to do. It was time to take his music somewhere beyond the local gigs where everyone else was performing.

One day, lightning struck. Otis was at home doing his chores and listening to WCHN, Detroit's premiere R&B station. The deejay, jive-talking "Joltin' Joe" Howard put out a call for anyone who knew Otis Williams of the (now) Siberians to call the station. Within seconds, Otis himself was speaking with another big-time local jock/producer Bill Williams, who wanted the group to record "Pecos Kid", which he had written after hearing the Olympics' novelty hit, "Western Movies." In a primitive make-shift studio in the basement of another air personality, Senator Bristol Bryant's home, Otis sang lead on "Pecos Kid" with "All of My Life" on the B-side.

Milton Jenkins, their manager, had a rehearsal space used a few times by the group, as well as by two trios - the Primes and their sister group, the Primettes. Many of the members of all three groups already knew each other from just hanging out in the neighborhood. As Otis described it to me:

> *It was Diane Ross at the beginning, and Mary* [Wilson] *and myself, we went to the same high school, Northwestern, as well as Melvin* [Franklin]. *Lamont Dozier, him and I went to the same junior high school and we would see Eddie Holland around the various record hops.*

Passing friendships aside, Otis immediately recognized that the Primes - Paul Williams, Eddie Kendricks and Kell Osborne - would kick his own group's butt in head-to-head competition. In his eyes, their performances reeked of class and sex, with awesome harmonies and slick choreography.

Bill Williams, for a short while their co-manager with Milton Jenkins, didn't feel he had enough time to devote to the group anymore, and recommended they contact a woman named Johnnie Mae Matthews, one of a large number of eager young entrepreneurs hoping to make it big in the music business. They began hanging and rehearsing at her house and anyone within earshot would hear the music and just drop in. One of the drop-ins was singer David Ruffin.

At about this time the name Berry Gordy, Jr. was starting to get street buzz. He had co-written a national hit, "Reet Petite", for a local guy named Jackie Wilson and was also known to be behind the embryonic success of the Miracles, whose lead singer was William "Smokey" Robinson, Jr. Those in the music business were beginning to take notice of Gordy, realizing this was probably someone who would make it big in the field.

Johnnie Mae formed Northern Records, recording Otis' group and other acts. She obviously had a good ear for talent, as one member of her roster was future Motown star Mary Wells. One group she recorded included a tambourine player/pool hustler named Norman Whitfield, who would later be a pivotal architect of the Motown machine. She also used a bass player in her sessions named James Jamerson who, like Whitfield, would achieve the same legacy status at the label.

Otis's group, now known as the Distants, found themselves in need of a strong bass singer and Melvin Franklin was recruited. With him came his close friend Richard Street to be the new lead singer. Within days, the five guys – Otis, Melvin, Richard, Al Bryant, and James Crawford- were in a studio at Specialty Records in downtown Detroit recording the up-tempo "Come On" and the romantic ballad "Always." "Come On" started making a little noise regionally and was bought from Johnnie Mae by the New York-based label Warwick Records. Shortly thereafter, James Crawford was out and Albert "Mooch" Harrell was in.

Wanting to capitalize on the small amount of recognition they were receiving, Johnnie Mae had them playing every possible jukebox joint and venue around town. While never having given any thought to the financial aspect of performing, Otis credits her for teaching them about the business side of things, and eventually he became the group's spokesman and go-to person when an issue arose.

By the summer of 1960, there were local dances everywhere, featuring lots of groups either singing their own record, if they had one, or covering the current hits. The Distants often shared a stage with huge talent on the order of Jackie Wilson, Smokey Robinson, and Eddie and Brian Holland. There was such demand for music, it wasn't unusual for Otis' group to finish one gig, hop in the car, and do one or two more in the same night.

Detroit's cup was running over with talent. Berry Gordy, Jr. had started the Tamla label on which he was recording such raw talent as Jackie and Smokey.

At this point, wasn't it about time for everyone to be under the same umbrella?

Yes, the time had come. And we all know that timing is everything in life, right?

> *We used to do record hops in and around Detroit. We were doing one at a place called St. Stephen's Community Center, and Berry was there with the Miracles, who were very hot at the time with a record called "Shop Around." My group, called Otis Williams and the Distants, had a regional hit called "Come On." We were doin' the record hop together, and my record was very, very popular in the Detroit area... so when we were on stage, we could see Berry come through the crowd with Smokey and the Miracles. And when we finished I'm standing there watching the Miracles, and Mr. Gordy was standing next to me and he just said, "Hey, man, we just have to go to the men's room," and there he said, "Hey, I like your group. If you should ever leave where you are, come see me. I'm startin' my own record company." I guess however many months later, I called him and came over to Motown.*

Once Otis and the guys became hooked up with the label, "Mooch" was booted because of his drinking and mood swings. So, too, was Johnnie Mae Williams. It's uncertain whether the Distants ever had a contract with her, but she was the money behind their four recording sessions on her label. To the shock of all, they discovered that Johnnie Mae owned their car, their uniforms, an unreleased song

Otis had written and...wait for it....their name! Suddenly, "Otis Williams and the Distants" existed no more.

Wisely, Otis was very careful about getting involved with anyone after being burned by Johnnie Mae. He was very taken with Berry Gordy – his personal manner and direct approach to business – so he lined up an audition with writer/producer Mickey Stevenson, head of the Artists and Repertoire (A&R) division at Motown. During the lag time, Otis heard from Eddie Kendricks, who had gone to Birmingham with his buddy Paul Williams. Both were back in Detroit and when the time came for that audition the two were part of the group. Paul had brought with him a great deal of experience in staging and dancing from the legendary Peg Leg Bates, and with his strong romantic baritone voice became the primary lead singer of the quintet known as the Elgins.

Things went so well that Gordy was called in to listen, and the group was offered their first contract on the spot. Finding out that there was another group out there calling themselves the Elgins, the guys bantered around names and opted for one which just popped into Otis's head: the Temptations. They laughed at the thought that, in their ragged outfits, they could tempt anyone or anything, but they figured it was an image they would try their best to live up to!

The years would prove they were right on the money.

In one of our interviews, I asked Otis to describe a typical recording session:

> *Well, it was fun, where we all recorded together...the*
> *Funk Brothers as well as the artists, meaning we'd all*

The Temptations
[Photo credit: Everett Collection/ Shutterstock]

be in the same snake pit, which is what we referred to as bein' in the studio. They had their little four-track recording and, you know, we had all these talented people in one studio and if one person messed up, everybody would have to stop and start over again. So it was a challenging task to record back then. We didn't think of it as other than hey, somebody messed up, let's go back and do it again. So sometimes it would get up to like Take 36, Take 40, 50, until we finally got it right. So it was fun making history. Little did we know we were makin' it, but it was great.

In addition to the rehearsals and recording sessions, Gordy wanted his artists to appear at their best on-and-off stage, so he asked them to attend his artist development classes taught by mentors about, among other things, how to dress and carry themselves at all times.

Well, they were like a school really. When we were on the road, sometimes they would start like ten, eleven o'clock in the morning, and we would have to be there until Motown closed, which was at six. They would give us an hour off for lunch and then we would come back. It was a very wonderful educational process about bein' in show business, and not of just relyin' on havin' hit records.

Otis Williams is the only original surviving Temptation, although many current members who are with him have been there for decades. The rest of the "classic lineup" of the group included Eddie Kendricks (lost to lung cancer at age fifty-two), David

Ruffin (died of a drug overdose at age fifty), Paul Williams (committed suicide at age thirty-four), and bass Melvin Franklin (passed away of heart failure at age fifty-two). During their decades of success, the lineup consisted of numerous performers, and the group always perfected a flawless succession of voices. At one time or another, you'd find Elbridge Bryant, Dennis Edwards, Ricky Owens and Richard Street. Others to follow included Damon Harris, Glenn Leonard, Louis Price, and Ali-Ollie Woodson (passed away from cancer at fifty-eight), Ron Tyson, Theo Peoples, Terry Weeks, Bruce "Bo" Henderson, Joe Herndon, and Bruce Williamson.

Williams has always credited the group's successful longevity to adjusting to the changing times without jumping on trends, and then being able to return to their older sounds. Juxtapose their Grammy-nominated first #1 Motown smash, 1965's "My Girl", produced by Smokey Robinson, against the Norman Whitfield-produced hits of the next several years - "I Can't Get Next To You", "Psychedelic Shack", "Cloud Nine", "Ball of Confusion (That's What The World Is Today)", and "Papa Was A Rolling Stone". In between those rough-hewn, spot-on interpretations of the state of the world, they effortlessly slid back into their earlier sound in 1971 with the #1 hit, "Just My Imagination". Sadly, Whitfield passed away from complications from diabetes in 2008 at age sixty-eight.

Chameleon-like, the Temptations have always been able to segue back-and-forth between a straight pop sound and a socially-conscious one of psychedelic soul, a distinction enabling them to rise above the majority of other groups of their era. Otis has often said he believes the Temptations are "God's Group." In our conversation, he elaborated:

> *I don't want to sound trippy or egotistical, but the history of the Temps and the many different person- nel changes we've gone through, we have been able to provide in spite of ourselves. I think there's been more damages we done to ourselves than any out- side factor could weigh in, and that's why I said this group is a very special group 'cause we should have been over and out a long time ago with the many dif- ferent guys we've had in this group. Through God's grace and our fan base and whatever, we've have been able to sustain ourselves and still be around.*

The '60s was a banner decade for Motown, as well as its affiliat- ed labels Gordy and Tamla. "My Girl" was a Grammy-nominated hit from 1965, and in 1968, the Temps became the first of Berry Gordy's groups to win the coveted award for Best Rhythm & Blues Performance By A Duo Or Group for "Cloud Nine". In 1989, Otis, alongside Dennis Edwards, Melvin Franklin, Eddie Kendricks, David Ruffin, and Paul Williams was also inducted into the Rock and Roll Hall of Fame. Four years later, "Papa Was a Rolling Stone" took home three trophies: Best R&B Group Vocal Performance, Best R&B Instrumental Performance, and Best R&B Song.

Otis Williams' memoir, *Temptations,* spawned a two-part NBC- TV movie, *The Temptations,* which chronicled the early years and their claim to fame. It netted a 1998 Emmy Award for director Allan Arkush. Two years later, the group won the 2000 Grammy for Best Traditional R&B Vocal Album for *Ear-Resistible,* and at the 2013 awards, they were honored with Grammy's Lifetime Achievement Award. On March 21, 2019 "Ain't Too Proud: The Life and Times of the Temptations", also based on Williams book, opened on Broadway to great reviews.

As of this writing, the Temptations have been making music for nearly sixty years – and they're not done yet.

*****

To the talented eager young singers of the transitional era, Berry Gordy's little house was seen as the opportunity of a lifetime. **Mary Wilson** certainly thought so.

Born on March 6, 1944, in Greenville, Mississippi to Johnnie Mae and Sam Wilson, she and her family moved first to Saint Louis and then to Chicago, where her father was able to find work. It was scarce, and although Sam was making a little money, it was coming in too slowly. Gambling, he believed, was the best and fastest way to be happy. Knowing how isolated, cash-poor and jobless Johnnie Mae was, her younger sister I.V. and her husband John L. Pippin, came to visit and assess the situation. They wound up taking their little niece back to Detroit to make things easier for her mother, leaving behind Mary's younger brother Roosevelt. Mary had no doubt that her mother loved her, but felt that she had lost control of her life, complicated by Sam's periodic appearances and disappearances. When Johnnie Mae was sometimes able to save a little money, she could count on her husband's taking it.

Mary, at the tender age of three, had no real understanding of what was going on, and pretty soon she forgot her birth parents and called I.V. and John "Mom" and "Daddy." She adored her house where she had her own bed bedroom, a beautiful lawn, a vacuum cleaner, and a freezer. Every year, John treated himself to a new Chrysler while I.V. drove around town in a Chevy. Perhaps the greatest treasures in the house, besides the aforementioned, were the 78 RPM R&B records her adoptive father kept in his wood-paneled basement. They ran the spectrum from Nat "King" Cole, LaVern Baker and Joe Williams, to Doris Day and jazz.

Mary was also lucky enough to have an adoptive mother who took great pride in how she dressed, and also clothed her niece to look like a little fashion plate. Mary loved it…except for the daily routine of having I.V. fix her hair, thru which she would cry her eyes out. Mary came to view this daily routine as an embodiment of her relationship with I.V. and began developing some traits which would not serve her well in future years, such as fearing authority and learning not to speak up when she felt the need. She worked hard on quietly trying to make I.V. happy, which was not easy because she was a no-nonsense disciplinarian, was very low on patience, and a perfectionist. She insisted on keeping an immaculate house, and always had to look her best in the finest clothes while making sure the entire family maintained and reflected her perception of quality.

Mary credits her daydreams, radio shows, and the movies, with transporting her into a world that would block out I.V.'s demands for perfection, and would teach her a lifelong lesson about maintaining peace regardless of the price she had to pay.

During the summer of 1950, Mary's life was altered forever. As she looked forward to the annual visit from her favorite aunt, Johnnie Mae, she learned the truth about her parentage.

The revelation that she'd actually been living with her aunt and uncle severely tested Mary's trust in people. By this time her birth mother, brother Roosevelt and sister Cathy ("Cat") were here to stay, and the three of them went to live in the southwest Detroit home of another relative. Birth father Sam Wilson was also back in the picture, and the family, after trying very hard to avoid it, was now living on welfare. They moved around a bit before settling in the Brewster Projects.

Mary couldn't have been happier! There were tons of kids, and the experience of having to get along with all kinds of people was not lost on her. In 1956, when she was in fifth grade, the city began busing students to various areas, in an early attempt at integrating the schools. It was in Ayers Elementary School that Mary met Carolyn Franklin, sister of Aretha and Erma, and attended their dad's New Bethel Baptist Church.

She never dreamed of becoming a singer; her fantasy was about becoming an actress who might someday sing. She was vocalizing just for her own pleasure… until she zoned in on rock and roll! She had heard Frankie Lyman and the Teenagers on the radio and had seen them on Ed Sullivan's television show singing doo-wop. That was all Mary had to hear! Studying the intricate blending of all the harmonies needed for doo-wop to work properly, she soon came to realize the difference between those sounds and singing solo or being in a choir chorus.

Musically, competition for attention and recognition was fierce; everyone chased the fame that the R&B and rock and roll pioneers were achieving. Despite the lack of a distinctive voice, Mary's aspirations knew no bounds. Parents in the projects never missed an opportunity to encourage their children to better themselves, bolstering their belief that there was no limit to their potential.

Mary had been content for a few years just to sing in the school glee club, and when she was fourteen, she impulsively signed up to sing in a school talent show. She decided to shed her naturally lady-like demeanor and shy personality to lip-synch to "I'm not a Juvenile Delinquent" from Alan Freed's movie *Rock! Rock! Rock!* She killed it! They loved her!

One of the other girls who performed was someone Mary knew from her neighborhood - a pretty, fair-skinned sexy girl named Florence Ballard, whom everyone called "Blondie". The two hung out at the end of the show, walked home together discussing their performances, and decided if either had the chance to join a singing group, they would do it together.

That opportunity came only a year later in 1959 when Flo was approached by a member of a trio calling themselves the Primes. Their repertoire included sounds that recalled the crooners who had been the teen idols of their heyday, as well as the teenage doo-wop that had become more and more pervasive. Managed and developed by Milton Jennings, they were looking for a "sister" group to present as part of their package. For the street-savvy, sharply-dressed, soft-spoken Jenkins, everything had to be first class and elegant; he would even chauffeur the Primes to their gigs in his red Cadillac. Money was king for him, and somehow he had the unerring sense that it was the music business that would be the ticket out of the inner city and its somewhat questionable entertainment venues.

Mary and Florence went to Jenkins' apartment to meet the Primes, who had moved in with their manager. Paul Williams thought his girlfriend Betty McGlown would be good for the group. There was also a fourth girl, one with big beautiful eyes, Diane Ross, another neighbor they knew from the projects. (She has said a clerical error on her birth certificate listed her as "Diana", but she called herself "Diane" until the Supremes became hitmakers).Quickly picking up the tunes and choreography the Primes had down pat, the girls became the Primettes. A visit to Mary's mom by the young gentlemen sealed the deal.

It was decided that nightclubs and bars were off-limits, but that sock hops and social club engagements were fine. Jenkins' girlfriend was to be their chaperone. Betty, the oldest of the group, lived in a different neighborhood, so they others didn't see her as often as they did each other. Mary, Flo, and Diane soon became best friends, each coming from a slightly different family background:

After experiencing a rather traditional upbringing while she lived with her aunt and uncle, Mary's life changed when her mother returned and reclaimed her. Gone were the rich furnishings, and fun parties in the basement with the wet bar, as well as expensive and chic dresses and a frilly blue bedroom.

Flo's family lived a life that believed in family first, sticking together no matter what, and keeping family matters private. Having given birth to thirteen children, (one of whom tragically died in an accident at the age of three), and enduring the death of her husband from cancer, Mrs. Ballard was determined to shield her children from danger.

Diane, the second of six children, also came from a close family - but unlike many of her peers, she had a live-at-home father. The Rosses believed that education was crucial, as was each child's personal achievement, and Fred Ross always encouraged his children to work toward their goals and fostered their self-determination.

Quite by chance the trio connected with a tall, lanky young guy they recognized from school who played guitar by the name of Marvin Tarplin. The combination of their harmonies and Marv's sound clicked, and he was immediately adopted as the fifth Primette.

Prior to Marvin's arrival, the Primes had been arranging the girls' songs, so none of the Primettes needed to read music. Tarplin was the only one with this skill, so having him with them singled them out as unique. No more need to lip-synch or pretend anymore; they were able to awe everyone by singing live at their gigs.

After months of constant rehearsals, including instructions from the Primes on stage production, handling cues, standing and speaking properly, the Primettes were ready for their first professional performance, at a large local union gathering. Under the watchful eye of Milton Jennings, who worked hard to get his "girls" opportunities to perform, they were booked for numerous teen dances. Becoming the best group around became their priority. Pretty soon Mrs. Wilson bought a sewing machine and Mary and Diane began picking out fabrics and making their own performance dresses. The more they practiced, the better their stage presence became. They took turns singing lead on the songs, but all that really mattered was that they excelled as a group, not as four individuals.

Keep in mind that when the Primettes were formed in 1959, Mary, Flo, and Diane were only in eighth grade! Moving on to various high schools, they continued singing while still living pretty typical teenage lives. As Mary told me:

> *We were only travelling on weekends because we were in high school, and our parents were, like, not really crazy about us singing. As far as they were concerned it was a hobby - something that kept us occupied - so they were very happy about that. And just being teenagers, all we had to do was do our homework, and wash the dishes or whatever our parents said, and we were free to do whatever we wanted to do. So they gave us total freedom in terms of saying, "You be home by eleven o'clock, or whatever you have to do, do it before you you leave." It was easy; and another thing...being teenagers, it was fun because we were doing something exciting. I hear a lot of other entertainers say, "Well, we became stars and we had no time for ourselves." But that was our time to ourselves. We enjoyed doing it.*

So did all this detract from the big things in school, like proms? Boys? Mary told me:

> *No, because, funny enough, a lot of times we would be the entertainment, so you know it was really great because we were these local stars and as far as we were concerned, it helped us to get to all the activities that were going on.*

I was curious as to whether she ever thought she'd be a bona-fide superstar.

I thought about being a star when I met Florence and Diane and starting in our group in 1959. But early on it was a little like an impossible dream.

As for dating…well, their mothers thought they were too young to "receive company", but as typical high school kids, the girls began channeling their hormonal urges into romances.

In early 1960, the girls' promising career took a detour. After the Primes stopped working with Milton Jennings, he seemed to disappear from the Primettes' lives as well. They had enough dates on their calendars to keep going for a while and began running their own rehearsals at Betty's house, building upon the foundation of direction and discipline their former manager had strongly instilled in them. But the immediate future turned out to be a real struggle for the four.

For one thing, Mary and Diane still had two years of high school to finish, but they were totally devoted to singing. Their times with Flo were pretty much limited to rehearsals, which were now being conducted by Flo's dear friend Jesse Greer. Impressed with how professional a musician Jesse seemed to be, Mary credits him with inspiring them and encouraging her to project her voice and take more of the leads while trying to get a less nasal sound from Diane. He also felt that Flo had great potential, as did the group, if only she sang more. Unfortunately, Flo seemed to be in the group more for the fun of it, lacking real inspiration to be a singer.

All the time spent rehearsing and perfecting their act finally paid off when the young ladies won first place in an amateur talent contest in Windsor, Canada. Shortly after, Marvin Tarplin passed along the message that the girls should go over to Motown. It was clear to them the only way to turn pro was to make a record, but it was easier said than done.

Even with misgivings about the business ethics of Gordy's company, they decided to go for it. Their "in" was supposed to be through Smokey Robinson and his Miracles, hoping if they auditioned for them first, someone would speak to Gordy on their behalf.

All went well and Smokey seemed to be on board – but his primary interest appeared to be in Marvin. Soon the Primettes would be without their accompanist. Once Smokey heard the guitarist, he snatched him up for himself. The two would go on to co-write some of the Miracles' and Marvin Gaye's biggest hits. Since Motown was still a work in progress, everyone connected to it was expected to play multiple roles. The Miracles were mentored by Gordy, who loved their enthusiasm and hard work, and Smokey had already begun writing and was even doing some producing. The girls had no doubt in their minds that having the guys both as friends and supporters, they, too, would soon be among those creating what has become known as the "Motown Sound" ever since.

It didn't hurt that when, in the summer of 1960, the young, determined, wanna-be stars went to audition for Gordy, they found a friendly face seated at the front desk, Janie Bradford, who they met earlier when they were with Milton Jenkins. Bradford would later become an important cog in the success of Hitsville, U.S.A.

With the brass ring close enough to be grabbed, the girls gave it their all, while Berry Gordy walked in and out of the audition.

He admittedly liked the song the group sang, but advised them to come back after they had all finished school. It later became apparent that business-wise he was still so early in building his company, the last thing he needed was the responsibility of four young females who were still minors.

It would be a cliché to point out that once someone doesn't get what he wants, his determination becomes stronger. Well, the Primettes were so enamored of the excitement and buzz within the building, that after their audition, they didn't want to leave. The fire under them to be part of Hitsville was stoked. And why wouldn't it be? Eddie and Brian Holland, who would be totally involved in creating the signature Motown sound were there, producer Norman Whitfield was there, and some of the label's biggest stars were hanging out as well.

Their self-confidence and obstinence became firmly rooted. The girls had no manager, but they decided to continue rehearsing at Betty's while they worked at getting their weekend performances booked at better and better clubs. They still continued to sing at teen gatherings. Most significantly, they would hitch rides to Grand Boulevard after school and spend their days just sitting around Motown. Convinced that Gordy would eventually sign them, they planted themselves in the building day after day.

Very quickly, Hitsville became the second home for would-be hit-makers. Family-style meals were still served to whoever happened to be there at mealtime. Close friendships and enduring relationships would develop there. Mary likened this to being in Disneyland:

> *I mean to sit there and see Marvin Gaye walk up and sit down and maybe play the piano in the outer studio there, or seeing Smokey Robinson run back and forth, hanging out with the Miracles...*

She underscored the uniqueness of the artists she was around and talked about how the company – producers, managers, and even secretaries – was like one big happy family, everyone on an equal basis.

> *Until* [the performers] *started making the hit records...then of course, they would become the big shots!*

Richard Morris was a recording engineer and musician who had been instrumental in getting the quartet their audition with Gordy and it was he who convinced Berry to let him work with the girls on the side in his free time. The daily rides to Grand Boulevard were no longer necessary as they rehearsed with Morris. In the girls' minds, this was just a temporary stop-gap until they hit the jackpot.

Once they hooked up with Richard and his friend Homer Davis, the picture brightened a bit; they were working all over the city, often at some of the larger, more established venues like the Graystone Ballroom and Twenty Grand, *the* premier nightspot. They weren't concerned that they were only the opening act for established performers like Wilson Picket and Johnny Mathis; they welcomed the exposure and the opportunity to perfect their act. Richard got along well with Mary, Betty, and Flo, but his patience was stretched when Diana dug her heels into whatever it was she wanted.

Mary viewed the Primettes as being of greater importance and larger than any of the members individually and was happy to be a team player. Diana didn't particularly share that vision, and as their career grew, jealousy, distrust, and competitiveness reared their ugly heads. While she was occasionally upset by what was happening, Mary shoved her unhappiness way down deep and kept her mouth shut. This was one of the coping mechanisms she had developed while living with I.V. as her mother. Mary believed strongly in "right and wrong" and that things would work themselves out; she feared if she said something, all of their dreams would be destroyed.

Late in the summer, Betty dropped the bombshell that she was leaving the group to get married. Compounding the shock and dismay at having to find someone to replace her, things took a turn for the worse when Flo seemed to disappear off the face of the earth.

Finally, Flo made the call and arranged to meet with the others. In a slow, agonizing, dazed monologue, she explained that after a show at the Graystone Ballroom weeks earlier, she had accepted a ride home with a guy she knew, and he raped her.

As a result, Flo retreated into her own world which she shared exclusively with her family. She was able to see her attacker convicted and sent to prison, but her self-esteem and self-image were shattered and she became prone to nightmares. After the horror she endured, Flo Ballad would be haunted by a lack of trust in everyone.

She slowly began to put the pieces of her shattered life back together again, first by returning to the Primettes and then by easing back into her school routine. With Flo's absence and Betty gone, the group's momentum had slowed, so they once again began working with Richard Morris, who continued to book them at sock hops and the Twenty Grand. Morris arranged for them to record at various studios, but their efforts, which were pressed and ready to be shipped, died a quick death in the midst of the infamous payola scandal. Numerous radio and record personalities were swept from their influential positions for allegedly giving or receiving payments for radio play.

Word had been out on the street that the Primettes were looking for a fourth member. One of Flo's music teachers recommended Barbara Martin, who passed her audition with flying colors. She seemed to get along with everyone, and smoothly filled the slot left vacant by Betty McGlown.

Great! Now they were ready for a full-frontal assault on fame! Except…their manager Richard was nowhere to be found. Apparently, according to Flo, he had been picked up on a parole violation. With this apparent setback, there seemed to be only one avenue to pursue: head back to Grand Boulevard and try and convince Berry Gordy that it was time to stop playing games and sign them!!

Their return to Hitsville was well received. By this time, Motown had grown and was becoming a well-oiled machine, thanks not only to Gordy's ear for talent, but his choice to surround himself with extremely talented singers, producers, managers, and family members. His devotees worked all hours of the day and night, excited and inspired by a man who clearly saw the big picture and exercised excellent judgment.

With this rapid expansion came a realization on Gordy's part that he would need to collaborate with others on writing new songs. So he began using people he felt could do the best job, and then pushed them to give the best they possibly could. He was extremely perceptive about others' talents and weaknesses and knew how to get what he wanted out of them.

One of the future superstars Berry had signed to the label was Mary Wells, who was both recording and writing songs. He decided to let the Primettes sing background vocals on a number of her tunes, or just be among the hand clappers in the back. Outside of that, their time was spent mostly sitting in the lobby, joking and making friends with only one object in mind: recording. At that point it wasn't really about the money or fame; it was strictly about making music.

By the start of the new decade, the stable of Motown artists and support staff had grown by leaps and bounds: Jackie Wilson, Smokey and the Miracles, Eddie and Brian Holland, Marv Johnson, and Lamont Dozier were on board. Even their old pals the Primes were part of the roster, as were the Contours and the gentle soul all the females had a crush on, Marvin Gaye. Martha Reeves, who was Mickey Stevenson's secretary in the Artists and Repertoire (A&R) department, also got her shot. Even Freddy Gorman, who had been the girls' mailman in the projects, brought Gordy a song he'd written called "I Want a Guy," and the boss finally gave the four of them the green light to record it. He also allowed them to work with Smokey.

Early in 1961, the Primettes heard the words they'd been praying for: Berry Gordy offered to sign them. Since the Primes were now the Temptations, Gordy saw no need for a "sister" connection any further and had them pick another name. From then on, they were the Supremes.

There were contracts to be signed of course, and like the Temptations, it never occurred to any of the girls or their parents to find their own lawyers. With their trust naïvely intact, they signed what was put in front of them, assuming Gordy and Motown would work on their behalf while serving also as their money manager.

Their new status as Motown artists upped the demands for their appearances at teen dances and other events. Without a manager, the girls were on their own as far as getting around from gig to gig, resorting to hitchhiking with the other artists. One of Gordy's friends from his boxing days, John O'Den, was now working at Hitsville and provided the girls not only with companionship but also chauffer services and, at times, covered minor expenses.

Nineteen sixty-one was an exceptional year for Motown. Berry was now filling his house with talented singers, writers, and musicians who would later become legends. The business end and support staff were hand-picked, and Mary still wonders how he had managed to find people who worked well below union scale. Smokey Robinson was upped to vice president, a position he held for decades. Thomas "Beans" Bowles, a sax player Berry knew from the Flame Show Bar, was having trouble making ends meet so he was lured in to help the company grow, as was Mickey Stevenson, a writer/musician who would become the supervisor of the company - setting schedules, arranging sessions, and enforcing deadlines. Barney Ales was the vice president of sales.

That summer, with Flo on lead, "Buttered Popcorn" became the second release on the Tamla label, a division of Motown. The company never promoted the recording; Mary found out later Gordy didn't believe it had the commercial sound he was looking for. At least now the Supremes had songs of their own to perform on their dates, rather than only covering others' hits. In Mary's mind, they were now finally legitimate.

Shortly after, the circumference of the girls' weekend itineraries widened. They were now hitting cities such as Cincinnati and Pittsburgh, traveling in John O'Den's van, and occasionally, on longer trips, in Gordy's Cadillac. This was the big time: they were accompanied now by house bands provided by the promoters, and sang just a few songs at each show, as did the other groups. Their first performance was on a bill with Gladys Knight and the Pips. Unfortunately, the Supremes bombed. Not used to singing without Marv Tarplin, the house band played in one key and the girls sang in another. Other shows, though, went as well as planned, but the girls were becoming less and less content with the local venues being booked for them.

Meanwhile, back at Hitsville, the girls were a constant presence. Everyone on the label seemed to be making that magical leap onto the charts: Mary Wells, the Marvelettes, the Contours, and the Miracles. The girls' release "Your Heart Belongs to Me" barely made the Hot 100, and "Let Me Go the Right Way" did slightly better, landing at #90. Now the Supremes were starting to worry, and even their biggest fans within the company were beginning to have doubts.

> *We were called the "no-hit" Supremes and it's amazing because we thought we were going somewhere. But everyone else started making records and really making their careers move forward when ours seemingly was not, because we could not get a hit record.*

[Finally,] *Mr. Berry put us together with the producing team of Holland- Dozier- Holland - that's Eddie
and Brian who are brothers - and Lamont Dozier.
And they have since been responsible for the music that was sung by the Four Tops, Martha and the
Vandellas, and of course, the Supremes.*

Mary had promised her mother that no matter what happened with
her career, she would finish school, and when she went to visit her
ailing father in Mississippi in the summer of 1961, she promised to
return the following year with a diploma in hand. Sadly, he passed
away a week before graduation.

That fall, Barbara stunned the group with the news that she was pregnant and left the following spring. At that juncture, the Supremes
decided it would be too much of an ordeal to try and find a replace-
ment, so they decided to continue on as a trio. Flo left temporarily
to tour with the Marvelettes and Mary and Diane floundered for a
while. However, Flo's separation and the subsequent days Mary and
Diane spent hanging around the lobby again were to be short-lived.
So would their "no-hit" status, despite the release of eight singles
that were total bombs.

The dam broke late in 1963 when the Holland-Dozier-Holland
composition and production "When the Lovelight Starts Shining
Through His Eyes" was released, and early in the following year,
it peaked at #23 on the Billboard Hot 100. Fourteen of their next
fifteen singles would reach the Top-10 (ten of them at #1) – and the
fifteenth peaked at #11. In August of 1964, their release "Where Did
Our Love Go" not only went to #1 but started a string of five consecutive chart-toppers. The song also peaked at #3 in the U.K., their

(l. to r.) Flo Ballard, Mary Wilson, and Diana Ross
[Photo credit: Dezo Hoffman/Shutterstock]

first single to chart across the pond. They were off and running, and the world was suddenly theirs – with devoted, adoring fans around the globe.

In 1967, Berry Gordy decided to change their name to Diana Ross and the Supremes, and that's when the lineup started changing as well.

Cindy Birdsong of the Blue Belles replaced Flo Ballard who tragically died of heart failure in 1976 at the age of thirty-two, just as she was getting her life back together. Jean Terrell joined the group after Diana Ross went solo in1969, and Birdsong was replaced in 1972 by Lynda Lawrence. The following year both Terrell and Lawrence were gone.

Mary, determined to keep the group going, reformed the trio, taking back Cindy Birdsong and adding Scherrie Payne. Four years later Birdsong left again, replaced this time by Susaye Greene. Under Mary's determined leadership, and after the departure of Diana Ross, the Supremes would chart fifteen more singles. "Up The Ladder To The Roof," "Nathan Jones," and "Floy Joy" were among their biggest hits on both the pop and R&B charts. "Stoned Love" was their last song to hit #1 on any chart in 1970.

In June of 1977, Mary faced the future and started out on a solo journey, touring Europe and Asia. The following year she, Karen Ragland, and Karen Jackson, the "New" Supremes toured England, where their fan base remained huge. But after a determined best effort, Mary disbanded the group and then legally lost the rights to the name "Supremes."

Her self-titled first solo album was released in 1979, and her second, *Walk The Line,* came out in 1992.

The original Supremes were inducted into the Rock and Roll Hall of Fame in 1988, with Mary accepting on behalf of the group. They received a star on the Hollywood Walk of Fame in 1994 and four years later, were inducted into the Vocal Group Hall of Fame.

Subsequent years have found Mary Wilson deeply immersed in humanitarian and global issue efforts. In 2003, she was named as a U.S. Cultural Ambassador by then-Secretary of State Colin Powell. She's a published author, an in-demand motivational speaker and supporter of an array of non-profit organizations. Mary has spoken out against landmines, served as a celebrity spokesperson for women's' health awareness, and has testified in front of various state legislatures in support of the Truth In Music legislation. This is a herculean effort to keep imposter groups from cashing in on the names and likenesses of famous groups, most of them from the seminal rock and roll era of the '50s and '60s.

One of her more current efforts is to maintain the legacy of the Supremes. She's done this by creating and curating a dazzling exhibit, "The Story Of The Supremes From The Mary Wilson Gown Collection." While promoting that effort, she has found time to write another book, "Supreme Beauty", and, like Gladus Knight before her, took to the dance floor as a contestant in season 28 of "Dancing With The Stars".

An extremely proud, vivacious mother and grandmother, Mary Wilson still performs and records today– still bearing that spark and determined grit to help others that she had sitting in the waiting room on West Grand Boulevard in Detroit so many decades ago.

CHAPTER 3
Los Angeles

Roughly 2,200 miles west of Detroit lies the city of Long Beach, California — where, on June 4, 1944 (a year after the arrival of her sister Russell Ann, a/k/a Rusty), **Holly Michelle Gilliam** was born to the former Joyce Leone Poole and Gardner ("Gil") Gilliam. They wound up living in Los Angeles.

Joyce died of a brain aneurysm when her younger daughter was only five, leaving her husband to raise Michelle and Rusty. Gil piled the two girls, books and bedding into his Plymouth and drove east to Buffalo, New York, where they stayed with one of his military buddies. Less than a year later, they re-packed the car to return home to L.A., where Gil re-married. Georgellen would be the first of five stepmothers for the Gilliam girls.

The marriage didn't last long, however, because Gil decided he wanted to go to college under the G.I. Bill. This little foray led them to Mexico City ... minus the second Mrs. Gilliam. After a period of adjustment, Michelle and Rusty learned to read and write Spanish fluently, and English became their second language. The trio remained south of the border until Gil's college experience ended after five years; then it was back to good old Los Angeles, where eleven-year-old Michelle was suddenly thrust into a whole new world.

Here, her peers were talking about things like boys, sex, their bodies, makeup, and clothes. She ran with a group of girls who hung out around a car club, then stuffed their beds with pillows and snuck out of their rooms after curfew. Life, for her, was to be lived in the here and now. Although there was no television in her house, there was a radio and lots of records. Her favorite sounds were Elvis and the early groups, like the Shirelles, the Drifters, the Everly Brothers, and any group produced by Phil Spector. She also dug the sound of black music.

Gil, who was very hip in his daughters' eyes, worked for Juvenile Hall at the time, and laid down the law to the girls based on what he saw there: they were never to get involved with hard drugs (although he didn't think marijuana was so bad), and were to observe curfews. He insisted that his daughters were not only going to get an education but maintain good grades as well. Still, Michelle admits that she and her sister knew more about sex and drugs by the time they were in their early teens than the average person would ever know.

In 1958, twenty-three-year-old Tamar Hodel would become the best friend of the 13-year-old Michelle, whom she called "a gorgeous little Brigitte Bardot." Tamar was married to Stan Wilson, a black folk singer with whom she had a child. It was through her that Michelle was introduced to the bohemian world of Josh White, Dick Gregory, and Odetta. She also got her first uppers and fake I.D. from Tamar.

The sound sweeping the country at the start of the new decade of the '60s was folk music. Clubs sprang up featuring both black and white performers, many of whom were considered subversive by "mainstream" Americans because of the political views expressed through the lyrics they were writing and singing. Comedians like Lenny Bruce, Mort Sahl, and Dick Gregory were also espousing the hot social issues of the day: the government, integration, and the role and rights of black citizens. At the same time, groups such as Peter, Paul and Mary, the Tarriers, the Weavers, and solo acts like Bob Dylan, Woody Guthrie and Pete Seeger were packing small, crowded night spots and occasional jazz clubs. Michelle and her buddy spent lots of time at San Francisco's hungry i, the Purple Onion, and the Trident.

Then, at age seventeen, Michelle's life path took a fortuitous turn.

One night, she and Tamar went to see comedian Dick Gregory, headlining at the hungry i. The opening act was the musical trio the Journeymen, consisting of tenor Scott McKenzie, banjo player Dick Weissman, and guitarist John Phillips. Tamar and Scott quickly became lovers and he moved in with the two ladies. Each night, John would come by to pick up his tenor for their gig and while Scott pulled himself out of Tamar's bed and got dressed, the tall guitarist with the strict military background and the blonde, high-spirited, happy-go-lucky flower child became friends.

> *When I met John Phillips I was a girl in love and I was not going to let this one get away. I thought he was adorable. He had a charisma about him ... he was obviously a leader and I just loved everything about him. We started a little romance in San*

Francisco but there were problems attached to it. He was married.

But did that stop the love-struck teenager? Not for one hot minute.

I made an appearance at his apartment and I met his wife. He had kinda disappeared and gone on the road and I hadn't heard from him. So this sounds insane ... I know she knew about me at this point ... and ... she was very nice to me. She invited me in and made me a tuna sandwich and a martini. But she said something that made me very suspicious. She said, "You know, I feel badly for you because John has a Michelle in every town." I didn't believe it, thinking this woman was workin' me here. Anyhow, John came back into town and he was furious that I'd gone to see his wife, naturally. He said, "I was in the process of getting a divorce." I said, "Well, you shoulda called." My father came up from Los Angeles and John convinced him that he should allow me to go to New York with him.

John was a very convincing guy, and he certainly gave the appearance to my father that he was going to take care of me, and that he was not going let my education lapse. And I think my father also realized that at this point I was seventeen-and-a-half years old. In six months, I was going to be able to do it anyway.

So with Gil's blessing, the couple took off for New York in early 1962.

Signing with John's agent, Michelle began a modeling career, thoroughly enjoying the money she was making on her own. She also started singing around the apartment with John, Scott, and Dick. It was tremendous fun for her; she never had any desire to sing professionally and there was no pressure at all. Whenever a fourth voice was needed, she happily joined in. When the three went on the road, John put his girlfriend into the Rehearsal Club, where she would live — supervised —with other teenagers who worked in some aspect of show business.

On December 31, 1962, John and Michelle tied the knot — and she chuckled as she recalled to me that besides John wanting her as his wife, he also wanted a tax write-off for the year!

By the following year, in John's absence, his new wife had begun an affair with a young singer/songwriter who had been dating her sister. Their relationship burned itself out pretty quickly and John, who had called his rival with a warning, took her back. The result of Michelle's straying? John's classic "Go Where You Wanna Go," the first charted hit for the 5th Dimension in 1967.

By 1964, it was clear to all that the Journeymen had started to fall apart. Michelle had been offered a job for $700 a week, but John encouraged her not to take it. Instead, he wanted her to join a new group he was putting together, which included Marshall Brickman of the Tarriers. Michelle took singing lessons in Sausalito, where they rented a house, and focused on traditional early English ballads. The New Journeymen, as they called themselves, began their professional career as an opening act at the University of South Carolina Homecoming and later opened for Bill Cosby in Washington, D.C. Still very unsure of herself as a singer at the time, Michelle credits John with giving her confidence and dimension.

With the players in place, the group took part in the Hootenanny Tour. One of the groups on the bus was the Halifax Three, which featured Denny Doherty singing tenor. Not long after that, Brickman decided to try his hand at writing rather than to continue singing, and the call went out that the rest of the New Journeymen were looking for Denny Doherty. This was a couple of years after John and Michelle, living in Greenwich Village, had co-written what would become their first charted hit, "California Dreamin'." Denny went to see the couple, and *voilà!* The songs they had been singing with Brickman sounded very different with the addition of a tenor voice, so they invited Denny into the group.

Continuing to perform on the road — well stocked with drugs, wine and beer — Michelle noticed that each evening Denny would be on the phone with his closest friend, Cass Elliot. Born Ellen Naomi Cohen in Baltimore, she had moved around quite a bit as a child, until her father encountered success in a business providing food for construction workers out of a converted bus which served as the kitchen. (She later referred to it as "Meals on Wheels for Schlemiels.") Cass was a hit in summer stock in a production of *The Boy Friend*. The applause was an aphrodisiac for the teenager, who dropped out of high school just before graduation to head to New York. After being on the road a while, she returned home to Washington, D.C. and enrolled at American University. Soon after, she, Tim Rose, and Jim Hendricks made a record for Warner Brothers as The Big 3. Then

Rose left, and Cass and Hendricks joined forces with Denny Doherty and Zal Yanovsky to become the Mugwumps. Later, Zal and John Sebastian formed the Lovin' Spoonful, and Cass and Denny became best buddies.

In her book *California Dreamin': The True Story Of The Mamas And The Papas*, Michelle notes that she and the others were so immersed in their folk music and their own little world, they were somehow completely oblivious to what was totally shaking up the rest of the country: the British Invasion. Once they heard the new sound coming from across the pond, they got caught up in it — and Michelle immediately sensed their own musical style would suffer. One evening, with Michelle's sister and boyfriend and Denny sitting around listening to the new Beatles album, they were introduced to a new drug that looked like a sugar cube. It was called LSD-25. At about the same moment as the drug kicked in, Michelle looked up to see Cass Elliot at her door, who consumed the strange substance as well.

Their whole world was now upside-down. The night was a first — simultaneously finding a new drug and a new friend. Michelle described the experience as the most incredible trip ever. She instantly took to Cass, who was five years older and her first "adult" female friend … one who was not only street-smart but also knowledgeable and independent. Cass encouraged Michelle to rely less on her husband and reclaim the total control he had over her life.

Shortly after that acid-enhanced introduction to the sound from the U.K., the group decided they needed some sun after traveling for four months. They spent ten days in St. Thomas, returning briefly to New York to fulfill the dates they had scheduled, before heading back to the sun, drinks, and drugs of the Virgin Islands. This time John, Denny, and Michelle headed to St. John.

And so began an adventure that, in a sense, marked the second phase of everyone's career. Life was fabulous: drinking, playing guitars, doing drugs, singing, and lots of sex. It was strictly living on the beach from day to day. Luckily, they could afford it. John was earning good money, as was Michelle with her modeling. But that wasn't all. Michelle had an innate sense that they were going to be successful, and there was no need to rush. "California Dreamin'" and "Go Where You Wanna Go" had been written, and the group was certain that they were developing their own style. They felt this little sabbatical was serving a purpose. John had become aware he could write music that had great commercial potential, and all that was needed was an entrée into the current music scene.

After a few weeks of camping out on the beach, Cass appeared out of nowhere one day — and the little flirtation between Denny and Michelle that was playing out right under John's nose intensified. It was also no secret that Cass was head-over-heels in love with Denny, although nothing ever came of it.

This reality of doing nothing but living and creating finally smacked them over their collective head. They were running out of cash and had to rely solely on Michelle's American Express Card. It was time to move on, so back they went to St. Thomas, where they hoped to find work. There they found Duffy, who owned and ran a boarding-house in the capital of Charlotte Amalie. Luckily, he had enough vacancies to enable the oddball group of troubadours to move in. In fact, he even built them a stage on which to sing for their supper. Cass didn't want to appear on stage with Michelle, due to the very obvious physical contrast between them. Instead, she opted to wait tables and sang the fourth part of the harmony from wherever she happened to be.

Money was still very tight, between what they owed for rent and food, among other things. So it was *sayonara*, Duffy (sorry we cost you so much to house and feed us) … *adiós*, Virgin Islands … and hello briefly to New York, before everyone was reunited out on the west coast.

Through their old friend Barry McGuire, they met record producer Lou Adler. Within two days, with $5000 and a car thrown into the deal, the group was signed to Dunhill Records, co-owned by Adler. Now they were in the big time!

Their "Monday, Monday" session included some of the top musicians available: the rhythm section was Larry Knechtel, Hal Blaine, Joe Osborn, and Phil Sloan — all members in good standing of the iconic session collective known as The Wrecking Crew. Engineering it all (as well as appearing as a musician) was future Grammy winner Dayton "Bones" Howe. As engineer and producer, he would later be associated with huge hits by the likes of Elvis Presley, Tom Waite, the 5th Dimension, the Turtles, Peter Tosh, and many others. "Monday, Monday" followed "California Dreamin'" onto the Billboard Hot 100 while the latter was still in the Top 10, making it to #1 in May of 1966; it was their only release to reach the top of the chart. Just after that single peaked, their first album, *If You Can Believe Your Eyes And Ears,* which contained the group's first two hits, spent a week at the top of Billboard's album chart.

The Mamas and Papas
[Photo credit: Globe Photos/Mediapunch/Shutterstock]

At the 1996 Grammy Awards, the Mamas and the Papas took home the coveted honor of Best Contemporary (R&R) Group Performance, Vocal or Instrumental for "Monday, Monday." They were also nominated in the Song of the Year, Best Performance by a Vocal Group, and Best Contemporary R&R Recording categories.

In June of the following year, heralding "The Summer of Love," the Monterey International Pop Festival took place. It became one of the most important events for the advancement and promotion of the international music scene. The event, which appeared to be the template for Woodstock two years later, embodied the counterculture of the late '60s, most typically the Haight-Ashbury area of San Francisco and Greenwich Village in New York City.

Brilliantly pulled-together in a mere seven weeks by John Phillips, Lou Adler, entrepreneur Alan Pariser, and publicist Derek Taylor, the spectacle drew, by some estimates, up to 90,000 people. The three-day seminal festival included every type of popular music imaginable, including pop, blues, folk, raga, and straight-ahead rock. Aside from the Mamas and the Papas, major attractions included Jefferson Airplane, Buffalo Springfield, Simon & Garfunkel, and Booker T & the MG's. The event also helped to launch the careers of Jimi Hendrix, Janis Joplin, Otis Redding, Laura Nyro, Canned Heat, Steve Miller, and Ravi Shankar. It was also the springboard for the Who to become a mainstream rock act in the United States.

The original Mamas and the Papas (named after what bikers called their women) were actually together for just a couple of years. They scored nine Top-30 hits between early 1966 and the end of 1967, with a final brief appearance on Billboard's Hot 100 in February of 1972. They also crossed over to the Adult Contemporary Chart in 1968 with "Dream A Little Dream of Me", credited as "Featuring Mama Cass with The Mamas & The Papas." Seven others of Cass's solo efforts also reached the Adult Contemporary Chart, including the song that precisely echoed the group's mentality, "Make Your

Own Kind of Music." The group was inducted into the Rock and Roll Hall of Fame in 1998.

Their time together may have been short ... but the drama that ensued was worthy of an Academy Award!

***

Another superstar who emerged from Los Angeles was **Darlene Love**. Born on July 26, 1941, she was the second of five children born to Ellen and Joe Wright. Joe held numerous jobs to keep his family fed; he was the assistant pastor at Pentecostal Assemblies of the World, which provided basically no income — so in addition to his church obligations, he did construction work on roads, cleaned buildings, and shined shoes on weekend mornings.

Being preacher's kids, the Wright children had strict limitations on their appearance and amusement within their home. Dolly (her mother's nickname for her) and her sister Edna began singing at an early age, and their voices were required to ring loud and true from the choir. (Edna later became lead singer of the Honey Cone, whose "Want Ads" was a #1 hit in 1971.) With a missionary mother and preacher father, only Gospel was permitted at home.

> *We couldn't listen to rock and roll, that's for sure.*
> *No rhythm and blues, no secular music was played*
> *in our house, and what I did, I think I listened to it*
> *outside of the house, 'cause all of our friends had it.*

Lest anyone get the impression it was all religion and nothing else, Darlene points out that she and her siblings were allowed to go to the movies and have lots of fun at home ... "balance," as she called it.

When Darlene was about ten, her father was offered the opportunity to become the pastor of a church in San Antonio, Texas. Leaving most of their belongings in California because shipping expenses would have been too high, the seven Wrights took a train to the Southeast. There were a great many pecan trees in their yard ... but that was about the only plus their new location had to offer. Their home was shabby and had no hot water until a collection was taken up so they could purchase a heater. Furthermore, the salary Pastor Wright was earning wasn't even close to the amount he needed to support his family, so for a few years he moonlighted as a printer and his wife cleaned houses. It fell upon young Darlene to assume the "mother" role in the house ... cooking, cleaning, and babysitting now all fell on her shoulders.

About a year after they arrived in Texas, the Wright family was in such dire straits that for a brief time, their children were sent to live with relatives. Darlene and Edna were "farmed out" to their father's sister Dorothy, in Port Arthur. Darlene later described her life there as "a nightmare out of Dickens."

During the five years spent down south, Darlene was coming to realize what a good voice she had. She had always sung in the church choir, but now she was enthralled with the voice of Marian Anderson and spent hours imitating her. Amazed at how good she thought she sounded, Dolly, now in her teens, started joining glee clubs at school and auditioning for solos at church.

When she was fifteen, the Wrights moved back to Los Angeles. Since they had departed five years earlier, the city had changed quite a bit. It now not only had the freeways that had been under construction last time they lived there, but to Darlene's delight, there was also the indisputable presence of rock and roll.

Pastor Wright didn't have his own congregation at the time, bouncing from one church to another on Sundays, but the family became members of a church where once again, Darlene was just another voice in the choir. One day, the director punished the teen for fooling around during practice and made her sing an entire song solo. She was so impressed with what she heard, she asked Darlene to come to a Christian bookstore and sing some songs during their radio broadcasts. Darlene credits that occasion as being the start of her "career."

Not long after, a girlfriend extended an invitation to Darlene that would change her life. One of the Blossoms, a popular backup group, was getting married and asked Darlene to sing at her wedding, as two others were doing.

> *They were looking for a girl to replace one of the girls in the group. And I actually auditioned to get in their group and I got in. One of the other girls was the lead singer, but when they heard my voice, they made me the lead singer. And from then on, we became the hottest backup group in Los Angeles.*

Initially, the girls were singing behind "mainstream" artists like Gene Autry and Doris Day, working their way up to Elvis, the Righteous Brothers, Ike & Tina Turner, and Johnny Rivers. Their voices were heard backing everyone from the Beach Boys to Cheech & Chong. Remember Bobby Day's "Rockin' Robin," "Johnny Angel" by Shelley Fabares, and Sam Cooke's "Chain Gang"? They were on those hits, and even sang on Bobby (Boris) Pickett and the Crypt-Kickers' #1 smash, "Monster Mash." The Blossoms were also friends with producer Lou Adler, who called the ladies in if the Mamas and the Papas were out of town or couldn't get to the studio, to enhance, or "sweeten" the sound of their music on songs like "Monday, Monday."

The Blossoms were on every producer's wish list. As Darlene told me in our Kool 96 interview, at one time, everybody wanted to use them.

> *One time we tried to do five sessions in one day, which is a total of at least three hours per session, and some were longer.*

After trading off driving following some long days and arriving home like zombies, the girls decided they would never do more than three sessions in a day — because there's only so much that human vocal cords can take, and further, they didn't have to. As union performers working under contracts from AFTRA (American Federation of Television and Radio Artists), they were making $22.50 an hour, with a minimum. Just as if they held down "regular" jobs, their income was steady.

> *Every week checks would come in ... they would stack up 'cause they had ten days to pay us.*

They were smart enough to stay current with their billing, keeping a written ledger of what was owed and when they got paid.

Darlene was in her last year at Fremont High at this time, and as popular as the Blossoms were becoming, they still took gigs at parties and sock hops, leaving them plenty of time to party and enjoy life as high school seniors do. She began dating a football hero three years older than her. Leonard Peete, who worked as an assistant manager at a grocery store. He won our heroine's heart and about a month before graduation, presented her with an engagement ring. They approached her parents and expected a firestorm from her father — but while Pastor Wright wasn't happy about the idea, it was *Mrs.* Wright whose disapproval shook the walls.

Darlene knew she had to get out of her parents' home. She was responsible for the cooking and cleaning, and was still the main object of her mother's rants and anger. She knew the only way out was to get married, and she was determined to do just that.

Then she got pregnant. She saw this child as her escape, and at a very early hour one morning, she and Leonard ran away. They needed to get his mother's approval since he wasn't twenty-one yet (girls only had to be eighteen), and the day they obtained it, they headed to City Hall and tied the knot. It wasn't long before the new husband began running around with other women.

Tragically, their daughter Rosalynn passed away when she was just a few days old. Before long, Darlene became pregnant again. The reality that kicks in after the initial bliss of married life got to Darlene, and music and her professional life gained new importance. The money that came into the house made it much easier for Darlene and Leonard to support their new, healthy son Marcus, who came into the world on March 11, 1961.

How nice to be versatile enough to be working all the time, making great money, and being so independent while still in their teens! The

Blossoms' styling, rhythm, and adaptability enabled them to sing any format. Only one of the singles they put out under their own name hit the Billboard Hot 100, although some of the songs were released by other singers later on and did chart, such as "Stoney End," a Top-10 hit for Barbra Streisand in 1971.

Among the producers with whom the Blossoms had done a few sessions were Herb Alpert, Lou Adler, and Lester Sill. It was a phone call from Sill, requesting a meeting with Darlene alone, that would change the course not only of *her* life and career, but would take pop music into an entirely new sound and direction. Lester Sill wanted Darlene to meet his partner, Phil Spector.

The fireworks were about to begin …

CHAPTER 4
Life On The Road

Members of The Supremes, Martha & The Vandellas,
The Temptations, and Smokey Robinson & The Miracles
[Photo credit: Ron Stilling/Shutterstock]

Cue the bullhorn: "Ladies and gentlemen of Motown, as you begin your very first road tour, we'd like to invite you to sit back and enjoy the air-conditioned, luxuriously appointed bus that's about to take you around the country as you perform on the Chitlin' Circuit. The restrooms are to the rear and if you'd like a snack from our small kitchen, please feel free to help yourselves."

Wait, WHAT??? Let's back this up a minute! Are you talking about this rickety, broken-down old bus? Is that even gonna get us around the corner? We're a bunch of young, fresh-faced, eager teenagers who plan to be superstars, remember? This is 1962, and we can't wait to hit all those famous black theaters: The Regal in Chicago … the Howard in Washington, D.C. … and, of course, the world-famous Apollo in New York! Those kinds of fancy-ass coaches and limos may be chauffeuring white performers around the country, but not us! The Temptations' Melvin Franklin described it clearly when he noted that any vehicle that had four wheels on it was a major improvement over the ones that carried the Motown Revue.

By 1964, the Temps were working and recording at Motown, the first company to package its own performers. The group also traveled in other caravans sponsored by promoters such as Dick Clark, Irving Field, and Henry Wynn, but their transportation situations were hardly any better.

The reality for the vast majority of black entertainers in the early 1960s was the harsh antithesis of luxury … or even the slightest hint of comfort. Sadly, their discomfort was not limited to their travel accommodations; it was also exacerbated by the racism and hatred they encountered.

Otis Williams noted that the three major forms of entertainment on the bus treks seemed to be sleeping, playing cards, and yakking with each other. The camaraderie this engendered was in large measure due to lack of any sort of personal breathing room. Do the math: each bus carried five or six acts, including chaperones, band members, and sidemen. Can you spell "cramped"?

On top of that, the itineraries weren't always well thought out, and some distances between gigs were hundreds of miles — sometimes with no free day in between. Williams recalled the number of consecutive days they would often have to go without a wink of sleep. While rolling through the South, they often had to stay on the bus. Even if they did find a bed for the night, it wouldn't be until a place could be found that would take black people — and those places frequently were rooms rented out by African-American residents. Many performers fondly remember Dick Clark as the one who would go into a restaurant and buy the food they would have to eat on the bus.

While some of the artists prayed only to get through their performances without screwing up, many were nervous just to be on the road, even with chaperones. This would be their first potential encounter with the segregation from which many of their parents had moved north to escape.

Otis Williams recalled that the reality was worse than they could have imagined, at least on the first tour, improving only as the years passed. As he elaborated to me on Kool 96:

> *Well, back then, the '60s were the most tumultuous decade in the last hundred years, and, you know,*

*the civil rights movement was at a very strong lev-el at that time. Dr. King was making his move, and all kinds of barriers was bein' brought up and torn down. We would run across quite a bit of that, you know. We were packing up our tour buses – this is the Four Tops and, you know, the Motown Revues – and these white guys came by and, you know, started sa-yin' n***** this...and shootin' and cussin' at us, and we all dropped to the ground. And never did I real-ize how many guns was bein' carried on the Motown tour, because us and the Tops, you know, we had to defend ourselves. But luckily it didn't get any worse than that. They just drove on off into the night.*

Well, you know, back then in those times, it was a bittersweet kinda feeling because we were naturally happy to be on the Motown Revue. We traveled all over the country and then there were times when we ran into, you know, the racial thing which was very, very prevalent back then. We were in South Carolina in this auditorium and there was a rope right down the center – one side blacks, the side whites.

Then we were in, I think, Kentucky — the Four Tops and we, the Motown Revue— and we had just fin-ished performing and we were loadin' up the buses and our cars and everything, and some white guys came by and they shot at us and called us the "n" word. And we all dropped to the ground and when we came up, we came up with guns and that kinda thing.

And then one time in Texas — ah, my home state you know — we were on tour again and we get off the bus to go in and [get] somethin' to eat, and we walk in and they say no, we don't serve the "n" word, and, ah, we had to leave there and go somewhere else to eat.

*****

Mary Wilson tasted prejudice even prior to the launch of the Motown tours. Just a week before her high school graduation, the teenager lost her father. When she went to arrange for the funeral service, she found herself in a Greenville department store in search of a pair of socks. The sales assistant treated her with such implied scorn that Mary was in shock. This was the first time she had been made to feel inferior because of her color.

It got worse in 1962, once she, Diane, and Florence were out on the caravans that began rolling south. Even their chaperones, including Mrs. Ross, couldn't shield them from the rawness. Perhaps the things that made these tedious sojourns bearable were the friendships and romances which grew out of, and inside of, the compactness of the vehicles. The presence of the veteran musicians, who usually claimed the rear area as their own, helped assuage the younger singers' concerns as they arose.

But they couldn't help the basic conditions. It was only on rare occasions that the troupe had a bed to sleep in (and never alone), or were able to take baths or do laundry. Black performers were rarely even allowed into restaurants ... and when they were, it was usually through the back door. After one show in Birmingham, Alabama, they were lucky to get out of town and out of range intact; they heard the crack of guns and later found bullet holes in their bus. Their welcome to Miami Beach, Florida was police cruisers and dogs, and the only reason one motel owner let them book their rooms was his desperate need of cash. In the ensuing decades, both the Temps and the Supremes would go on to be treated like royalty. All hail "The Sound of Young America," as Berry Gordy liked to call his minions.

*****

Gladys Knight's eye-popping experiences were similar, yet strikingly unique. Granted, the Motown artists who hit the road had hairy stories to relate, but for the most part, they were in their later teens. Gladys started touring with the Pips when she was just eight years old. While the guys tried to keep life's humiliating and uglier side from the youngster, she witnessed and heard a lot, which made her feel very vulnerable and had her yearning for her quiet, more protected life back home. She believed that had she not been exposed to life on the road at such a young and vulnerable age, she probably wouldn't have had to face the blatantly ugly, heartbreaking experience of racism until she might have been better equipped to deal with it.

The truth is that when she won the grand prize on Ted Mack's show, some of the white contestants and their parents showed their resentment by refusing to pose with her for publicity shots. As she explained to me on Kool 96:

> *When I think about it now, I say "Whoa!" because*
> *I was so green. I was so innocent. And in my fam-*
> *ily, we weren't raised with that element. It's like, we*
> *don't judge people, and if someone does you wrong,*

just deal with that person for what that person did to you or did not do to you. You know, it wasn't whether they were black or white or what-have-you. When I went on the show and the parents were a little bit ticked, I mean, it wasn't a widespread thing to have an African-American on TV during the '50s, come on now. So they weren't happy for me. I was just a little stunned by that. I would have been happy for them if they had won.

During this era, dozens of other black performers would try to book accomodations on the road, only to be met with "No Rooms" signs … hotels, motels, it didn't matter. The message was clear: black people were definitely not welcome there. In her book *Between Each Line of Pain and Glory,* Gladys related a story of being thirteen years old and needing to use the restroom at a gas station while on the road, only to be told that n*****s were not welcome to use the facilities. Of course, they were more than welcome to spend money inside and make any purchases they wanted!

One traumatic experience took place in Little Rock, Arkansas, when she and the Pips had to perform twice — first for a white audience, and then for a black one. The greatest insult of this particular stop was finding a hotel that would book them rooms … until they got kicked out.

One of the biggest and ugliest truths Gladys learned on this trip was that just because some people wear badges and uniforms, they're not always the good guys. It seems the police chief didn't want any blacks in his town overnight, so he gave them a very short time limit within which to leave the hotel and get themselves on the road again. Once they had hastily re-packed the vehicle, they got police escorts — sirens screaming — to make sure that the city was in the rearview mirror of their bus.

On another tour with Smokey Robinson and his Miracles, Jerry "The Iceman" Butler, Chuck Jackson and assorted other acts, they were hauled in by the cops, who proceeded to take the men's jewelry and wallets before arresting them. So you want to be a superstar, huh?

Such experiences weren't limited to people of color. The Mamas and the Papas, known for their civil rights and political action crusades, got the last laugh when they showed up for a gig in Alabama.

A pair of purported representatives from the NAACP told John Phillips that there was a request to cancel the show because promoters were allegedly refusing to sell tickets to people of color. Boy, did they pick the wrong group! That may have been a commonplace occurrence down there, but the group would have none of it. They immediately canceled the show and left ... and proceeded to perform at a black college shortly thereafter!

CHAPTER 5
The British Invasion

Unlike the warning of impending danger that residents of Lexington, Massachusetts had as Paul Revere rode through its streets in 1775, mainstream America had nothing as dramatic to alert it that the British were coming again nearly two hundred years later.

By the late 1950s-early '60s, blues and rock-and-roll pioneers like Elvis Presley, Roy Orbison, Little Richard, Buddy Holly, James Brown, Muddy Waters, and Chuck Berry had caught the ears of British teens. Since their previous primary musical influences before then had been Celtic, music hall, Mersey Beat, and skiffle, they went as wild over the new beat and lyrics originating across the pond as their American counterparts.

British artists worked hard to capture the essence of American rock-and-roll, and by the close of the 1950s, they seemed to finally grab hold of it. In 1963, Dusty Springfield became one of the earliest U.K. singers to break onto the American charts with "I Only Want To Be With You." The following year, the tsunami known as the Beatles washed up on our shores. Suddenly, the pop charts were inundated with new names: the Rolling Stones, Herman's Hermits, the Animals, the Yardbirds, the Dave Clark Five, the Kinks, and many more.

This became the death knell for many home-grown American artists and groups whose names had preceded the newcomers on the sales charts. Suddenly a British accent had become a prerequisite for success in pop music.

Chuck Negron, like many other musicians, tried to make sense of the new world order.

> *All these writers that came out of New York, just had owned the charts — and all of a sudden, the Beatles came in and changed everything. Everyone was writing. All these writers needed a place ...someone to do their material. So I knew if we [Three Dog Night] could tap into this, we would have a plethora of the best. And that's exactly what happened, because they had no place else to give them. Everyone else was trying to write. So I knew that we were in a good moment in time, and we could do what wasn't being done at that time. Of course, we did get some flak for it because they said we did other peoples' stuff, but we did exactly what was going on in the business for years before the Beatles.*

One of the first definitive sounds to exit the scene was that of the girl groups: for example, the Shangri-Las reached the Billboard Hot 100 only from 1964 to 1966, the Crystals were hit makers from '61 till '63, the Chiffons had their smashes between 1963 and '66, and the Shirelles stayed strong from '60 to'63. Some of the Motown girl groups lasted a few years longer; Martha & The Vandellas were big from 1963 to 1967. The major exception was the Supremes, who were in demand worldwide well into the '70s, both with and without Diana Ross.

Motown male groups also forged ahead: the Temptations were still charting into the '90s (with Rod Stewart on "The Motown Song"), and even released a new album in May of 2018. The Four Tops managed to do likewise into the late 1980s.

Tin Pan Alley teams such as Jerry Leiber and Mike Stoller, Doc Pomus and Mort Shuman — and married couples like Barry Mann and Cynthia Weil, and Ellie Greenwich and Jeff Barry — who had so skillfully and successfully crafted tunes that resonated with teens and young adults, now found that there was a total disconnect. Everything was affected: Mary Quant and the Mod movement replaced poodle skirts and bobby socks, and angular Vidal Sassoon-inspired hairstyles and Beatle-style mops were the final nail in the coffins of beehives and crew cuts.

For Ellie Greenwich and her colleagues, it was a rough time — although she turned out to be one of the luckier songwriters who endured the deluge.

> *It was a very scary time because, I mean, the girl group thing was like "See ya!" Although I must say for me, as scary as it was, I had two little incidents that were wonderful for me: "Chapel of Love" came out on the Red Bird label and the headline in one of the trades was "'Chapel of Love" Breaks Through*

*The British Invasion," and then Manfred Mann re-
cords "Do Wah Diddy Diddy." So it was kinda
like, "oh, it's not so bad"...but after that, it was
"okaaayyy ... now what?" It was a very, very scary
time for us — it really, really was. I think a lot of us
[were] trying to find our own, as we say, "vehicles,"
for you, the writer/singer person, to get out there and
do their thing. And fortunately for us, Neil Diamond
happened to come along, and a lot of effort was put
into his career. So, you know, we produced all his
early hits and stuff. It worked out fine, but it was the
end of the girl group era. It was the end of what we
were so used to doing.*

Fortunately for Ellie, her versatility would enable her to be prolific
for many years to come.

*****

But the end of the era during which Darlene Love made tons of money as a background singer with the Blossoms saw her career grind
to a screeching halt practically overnight. No longer did the magic
from the successful songwriting teams on which the girl groups had
relied resound down the halls of Tin Pan Alley. A few managed to
linger a tiny bit longer; the Dixie Cups became the first American
group to land at the top of the charts in 1964 with Ellie and Jeff's
"Chapel Of Love." For the record (no pun intended), Darlene was
the lead voice on the original recording of that song. Her voice was
also heard headlining other hits, including the Crystals' "He's A
Rebel" and "He's Sure The Boy I Love." Thanks to Phil Spector,
her lack of label credit made it extremely difficult when she was

trying to re-start her career, and it was not until many years later that she received the acknowledgment and financial compensation she deserved.

That said, in time Darlene not only resurrected her career, but in 2011, she was inducted into the Rock & Roll Hall of Fame. Three years later, *20 Feet From Stardom*, a film highlighting the careers of Darlene and other unheralded background singers, won the Academy Award for Best Documentary (Feature). That, however, was hardly her first foray into movies; many people didn't even recognize her when she appeared as Danny Glover's wife in the *Lethal Weapon* films!

Darlene's subsequent success has created such a demand for her performances that even she is astonished. In 2015, she released her first non-holiday studio album in 17 years, produced by Steven Van Zandt of Bruce Springsteen's E Street Band and the TV blockbuster *The Sopranos*. She continues to perform regularly, having finally come into her own after six decades of making music.

*****

The British Invasion also took a tremendous toll on Neil Sedaka.

Along with Elvis, Fabian, Bobby Rydell, Paul Anka, and a handful of other handsome teen idols, Sedaka initially hit the charts in the second half of the 1950s. By the time the Beatles first appeared in 1964, the Brooklyn native could brag about seven Top-10 hits, including his chart-topping up-tempo observation that "Breaking Up Is Hard To Do." (A slower version of the tune peaked at #8 on the Billboard Hot 100 in February of 1976, and hit the top of the Adult Contemporary chart that month as well.) Surprisingly, his songs were sometimes even more popular abroad than in the United States. "Oh! Carol," his after-the-fact love letter to high school girlfriend Carole King, made it to #9 in the U.S. and #3 in the U.K.

And why was that? He told me on Kool 96:

> *I think that the English and the Europeans had a lot of respect for the original rock and roll American singers. They were very big over in the U.K., and I think they kinda of fantasized overseas about the teenage life, and about the doo-wop music, and about New York City — all the original rock and roll things. They saw it and they read of it, and kind of fantasized about it.*

So began an entirely new part of Neil's life.

> *Oh, people came up to me in New York and said;*
> *"Didn't you used to be Neil Sedaka?"*

Thanks to his enormous and multiple talents, work didn't cease altogether for Neil — but this fork in the road compelled him to change his focus for many years to come.

> *I stopped singing for ten years. Actually, I wrote for a publishing firm, and it was a nice time, 'cause I was able to sit back and stay home, and Leba and I had a family. We had two children, and I lived in Brooklyn, New York for those few years. I wrote for Johnny Mathis, Andy Williams, Elvis Presley, Karen Carpenter, Peggy Lee, the 5th Dimension, and*

others. But you know, Claire, if you're used to be-ing on a stage singing yourself, there's nothing as exciting. And it was during those years that I kept thinking perhaps, maybe, there's a chance for me to record again.

What was the clue that the time was right to try moving to England, and begin performing there, as he subsequently did?

A very dear friend of mine, Dick Fox, who is an agent, said that I should go over to England and try for a comeback. The American disc jockeys watched the English charts very carefully. They saw that I was having Top-10 records with [the British group] *10cc. ...it was kind of a mellow rock time in the mid-'70s.*

Taking Fox's advice, Sedaka made the journey with the hope of getting his American career back on track.

It was kind of humbling, 'cause I had to start in the workingman's clubs, and there were only a few peo-ple in the audience. Believe it or not, Leba, my wife, worked the lights. People wanted to hear "Happy Birthday, Sweet Sixteen" and "Calendar Girl," but I was able to sing some new songs, and then I got an offer to do Talk Of the Town [a popular upscale club], *and then the Albert Hall.*

Sedaka was able to slowly re-build his reputation and a foreign fan base. He released three albums in England but had absolutely noth-ing going on for him in the States. Thank heaven for Elton John, who felt Neil was destined to be the next great American superstar, and signed his friend to a new label he was starting, called Rocket.

Slowly but surely I gained a great reputation in the U.K., and it finally trickled across the Atlantic, back to America.

By the mid-1970s, two of Sedaka's Rocket releases, *Sedaka's Back* and *The Hungry Years,* both had gone gold. "Laughter In The Rain" got him back to #1 on the American pop and adult charts, and "Bad Blood," his duet with Elton John, also topped the Hot 100. The icing on the cake was when The Captain & Tennille's version of "Love Will Keep Us Together" was named Billboard's #1 Song Of The Year and won the 1975 Grammy for Record of the Year. As Toni Tennille ad-libbed at the end of the song, "Sedaka is back!" Indeed he was.

Ironically, the country that previously had turned his world upside-down embraced the singer and helped resurrect a career that is still being honored around the world today.

As we have seen, the British Invasion had both positive and negative repercussions for American music. Many songwriters and composers needed to find a new direction to pursue, as Chuck Negron noted, and some just fell by the wayside. The Beatles had ushered in a new era ... one in which artists became more self-sufficient, and were writing and recording their own lyrics rather than relying heavily on others to craft their words.

On the flip side, though, it was also a great opportunity for unheralded writers like Laura Nyro, Leo Sayer, and Randy Newman to find outlets for their work, for groups like The Mamas and The Papas to be heard, and for folk singers who had been on the periphery of the mainstream music scene to have a greater say in the sound of the era. For Chuck Negron, it all harkened back to the Brill Building, where he hunted for new material.

> *We were at the Brill Building three days a week, going to hundreds of offices, you know, trying to get them to sign us to get some songs. So at any rate, when Three Dog Night came together, I said, "You know, now I have some muscle, 'cause I couldn't get a song back then." And I went in and met these guys — that's how I got Harry Nilsson, that's how I got to Paul Williams, Laura Nyro ... one of the publishers played [her], and I said "I know Laura." And you know, boom! I was off! In the first album, I think I have about five or six songs that I brought. I wanted to go with newly-written stuff. It worked for us.*

So just how did Chuck manage to pick material that would put his group onto the charts?

> *I think that's something in you. I think that's something that's a combination of things; it's a part of being in tune with what's going on, having a part of you that's creative, and having some taste. Plus ... this is the difference between me and a lot of people that picked songs: having the ability in the range to not mentally limit a song. "Oh, I can't do that, because there's too much range." And people do that. I had no limits on what I could do, 'cause at that point I*

had a four-octave range, and at times on stage, I had over a five-octave range when I was warmed up. So my mind was open to whatever was out there. And you know what? I know now, I didn't know it then — I had a great ear. Because you know, I picked a lot of hit songs. I mean, "Joy To The World" was turned down by everybody in the band [and] our management. We had started a production company and [lyricist] Hoyt Axton, to whom I brought the song five times, hired someone to bring it in for him and they turned it down. Hoyt came to the studio one day and played a couple of songs and said, "I'm gonna sing that song again." And the guys went, "Oh, no." And he played it, and I went "That's a hit song. I'll do it."

Chuck's ears did not deceive him. Nine months after Three Dog Night had topped the Hot 100 with "Mama Told Me (Not To Come)", they did it again for six straight weeks in the spring of 1971 with "Joy To The World."

CHAPTER 6
Love Is Color Blind

During the years, the Supremes were starting to grab international attention and Darlene Love was unknowingly recording for Phil Spector under numerous aliases. She still continued her backup work with the Blossoms, while nationally...well...things were a-changin'. As described in the previous chapter, the initial rumblings of the British Invasion brought tidal waves of new, exciting artist-written music to us, effectively ending the girl group era and the careers of numerous pop singers whose sounds just weren't appealing to America's record-buying public anymore.

What *was* happening was turmoil in every aspect of life in the U.S.: John F. Kennedy was elected president - bringing energy, hope, vitality and the magical dream of Camelot to the White House and beyond. That ended in Dallas in 1963.

Three months earlier, Dr. Martin Luther King, Jr. held his March on Washington, with over two hundred thousand peaceful demonstrators listening as he spoke of justice, equality and his dream for all Americans. The following year, at thirty-five years of age, Dr. King became the youngest person ever awarded the Nobel Peace Prize. Racial discrimination issues were front-and-center in the consciousness of Black America, fomenting demonstrations, and bringing forth new leaders to fight the fight.

In March of 1965, President Lyndon Johnson initiated Operating Rolling Thunder, air strikes on targets throughout North Vietnam, representing a significant escalation of U.S. involvement. Although he was likely unaware of it at the time, Johnson's actions would reverberate for decades. To paraphrase the title of Neil Sedaka's 1973 album, the "tra-la days" were definitely over!

While African-Americans were fighting for equal civil rights, interracial socialization and dating were very touchy and often taboo issues for the population at large. However, in show business - especially in the world of music - it was very common for black and white performers to become not only very close friends but lovers as well. They just were careful not to flaunt it.

As happens all the time when you're a superstar, people want to meet you. Mary Wilson was used to being pursued by dozens of guys, even other celebrities, who wanted a chance to date a Supreme. In 1967, there was a concerted effort on the part of Norman Wise, the group's booking agent, to fix her up with another superstar, Tom Jones. He'd been trying to get the two of them together in the past and for some reason this time Mary went along with it. She'd heard of the handsome new singer and had bought some of his records... only to be shocked that he was, in fact, white.

They agreed to meet in Munich, Germany at an awards ceremony. "Giddy" is how she describes herself as the time drew near. Having dated a number of men since her romance with the Temptations' Duke Fakir ended, she was ripe for a new rendezvous.

The night of the Supremes' first show, there was a knock on their dressing room door... and there he stood in all his tuxedoed Welsh glory. Instantaneously the sparks flew.

Following the performance there was the usual grand celebration at the hotel. Mary felt the electricity of Cupid's arrow...this was love at first sight for her, and the attraction was obviously mutual. She was certainly aware of his reputation as a womanizer; she soon realized that despite his relatively new-found fame, here was a man who spoke his mind without hesitating and had values in synch with the average working class. She loved both qualities.

The two were compatible on every level possible as friends and lovers. Their hectic schedules allowed them to be together on a hit-or-miss basis, and they piled air mileage up the wazoo flying to meet each other no matter where in the world they were.

Then came the shock of all shocks: Mary found out that not only was Tom married, he also had a child. The rest of the world had known, but Mary apparently had been oblivious.

Following her experience with Duke Fakir, who had also been married during their affair, she vowed that she would only date men who were available. She had every intention of breaking up with Tom... but quickly realized it would be hopeless to try...it was just too late to walk away. She was young, in love, and hopelessly invested in the relationship.

Life was blissful when they were together; they laughed, talked, made love and enjoyed every magical moment, despite her being portrayed in the fan magazines as being the one tearing apart Tom's family. They were seen out together by the press and word of the affair had gotten back to Motown, but no one ever made mention of it.

Mary knew she was between a rock and a hard place; while, ironically, she admired fidelity, she realized that Tom would never leave his marriage. This was driven home when the two were in a cottage Tom owned in England. His suspicious wife called, saying she was coming. Poor Mary was sent shuffling back to London alone. Meanwhile, she was also well aware that that love of her life had legions of female followers, who threw their underwear and themselves at him every chance they got. Would they be in his bed when she wasn't?

This woman who was chased by adoring men, who would have given anything to be with the man known to friends and fans alike as "Tiger", knew the situation was hopeless. It had to come to an end. The intensity of their feelings was so great they couldn't keep their globe-trotting romance going.

Finally, the end did come at a party Mary threw in her Hollywood home. She carried a flame for him and hoped against hope that perhaps things might work themselves out…but it became clear after one of the Supremes performances, that such a reunion would never happen. Tom came backstage to see Mary…and introduced his wife. That was the final nail in the coffin of a once wild, exhilarating, whirlwind affair.

To this day, Tom Jones and Mary Wilson remain very close friends.

*****

As noted previously, Darlene Love and the Blossoms were the prime backup singers in constant demand for work. One of the sexiest, hottest acts of that era was the blue-eyed soul duo of Bill Medley and Bobby Hatfield ...better known as the Righteous Brothers. How hot? In just fourteen months, between the end of 1964 and March of 1966, they had five consecutive Top 10 hits (and were still on the charts into the '90s).

Jack Good was a producer Darlene and the girls met while backing Jackie DeShannon in England. He had a dream of bringing to America a cutting-edge TV show that was similar to what Dick Clark was doing on *American Bandstand*, but unlike Clark's program, it would feature artists singing live. The template would be the British show *Ready, Steady, Go.* This new production, called *Shindig,* joined ABC-TV's lineup in September 1964. Good was a devotee of black music, and many of the featured acts were African-American, although some white artists became regulars. One of those was the Righteous Brothers, a group not unfamiliar to Darlene.

> *We had recorded with the Righteous Brothers long before they became famous 'cause we were doin' all their hits long before they came on Shindig. They made the Righteous Brothers and the Blossoms like regulars on the show. And while on the show, they met Phil Spector and recorded "Lovin' Feeling". And what they would do...on the weekends... they would go out on the road and, you know, work on their hit. And the Blossoms, it was so funny because*

we were stuck on Shindig...not so much stuck, but that was our regular job for about two years, and we weren't even goin' out on the road.

When the TV show ended, they did finally travel with the guys.

You know, because knowing them the way we did, we never talked about what they were doing on the weekend when they weren't doin' Shindig. And we went out on the road with them; it was like "You guys are stars!" They were playin' to rooms that's holdin' 10- 20,000 people. People at that time during the '60s weren't playing rooms that held, you know, so many people. They're doing that today, but that was unheard of back in the '60s unless you were the Beatles. The Beatles came out and they were playin' baseball fields. So for the Righteous Brothers to be playing rooms that held 10 - 20,000 people, it was truly amazing to the Blossoms. I don't even know if Elvis did that. No, I know he did not in the '60s.

During this time, Darlene became more than Medley's backup singer. Both of their marriages were on the rocks, and she was both lonely and depressed as the Righteous Brothers crossed over from being one-hit wonders to certifiable stars. Her career didn't seem to be going anywhere fast, and she began to have doubts about whether stardom was really what she was really looking for.

Too keyed up to go to bed after their shows, the two would take long walks ...seemingly lost souls trying to make sense of the world around them. Darlene says she had never thought of being in a relationship with a white man, but with all their talk, silly antics and alcohol-fueled horseplay, she felt herself falling in love with Bill. To keep the atmosphere light, they would lob "black" and "white" jokes back and forth at each other, in anticipation of any racism they might come up against.

One night when they got to Darlene's bedroom door, they finally crossed the forbidden line. Bill's tenderness and compassion was a real eye-opener for her. They kept their affair under wraps as they traveled together, always registering for separate rooms, and later finding each other in the dark. The members of Bill's band began to notice a change in the lanky singer and kidded him about the stars in his eyes. And then, one night with her by his side, the singer who never met a bottle he didn't like…often to excess…confessed that he was in love with Darlene.

The relationship was a long, serious one, immortalized on the Bill Medley 1968 solo single "Brown Eyed Woman," on which Darlene sang backup. In his memoir, Bill tells the story of songwriter Barry Mann coming over to play him a new song, saying, "I've written a song but I need to explain it to you. Now listen, this has never been done, it's about a white guy in love with a black woman. He's saying, 'I love you," and she's saying 'Stay away, baby." Are you willing to take that risk?" At precisely that point, Darlene came walking out of the kitchen – and Mann said, "I'll take that as a yes."

Mann added, "When Cynthia [Weill] and I wrote the song, we had no idea that Bill and Darlene were dating. When we played them the song, Darlene actually thought we knew about it and had written the song especially for them. It was a hit in New

York, L.A., and Chicago, but they wouldn't play the record down south." Darlene:

> *It was three years... and the other part of that was that unfortunately, a lot of people around us didn't like it. They're out there and everything is so wonderful and then you find out they ain't so crazy about you* [being in an inter-racial relationship]. *You know people aren't as open-minded as you think they are.*

So did they contemplate making their relationship more permanent?

> *Oh, yes, it got to a point where we were very, very serious. But then he let me know that he thought my career...you know... that I would stay at home, and that I wouldn't sing anymore. And I said, "Well, what would I do if I stayed at home?" I'd been singing since I was sixteen. What would I do?" I could see my life really changing and I didn't know whether it would work. And then Bill was starting to become very possessive... another thing that wasn't working too well with us bein' in this business. Slowly but surely, you know, he went one way and I went another way.*

They've remained friends ever since, even appearing as themselves on the now-defunct soap opera "One Life to Live" in 1994, singing "(You're My) Soul and Inspiration." Bill says, "There's a humanity that comes out of Darlene's voice that is just so real – she's one of the best singers in the world. She's also one of the greatest people I know."

Darlene Love and Bill Medley at the
5th Annual Right To Rock Benefit, New York City

CHAPTER 7
Abusive Marriages

Lights! Camera! Action! No … *wait!!* No action yet, Mr. DeMille, and definitely no camera. These ladies are in no way ready for their close-ups! Can we get makeup in here, please?

At just-turned-eighteen, Darlene was a high school senior and, perhaps more importantly, pregnant. She and her boyfriend Leonard Peete tied the knot, and her work with the Blossoms was relegated to the back burner as she became a wife and prepared to become a mother. Her husband began running around early in her pregnancy; in fact, it was very difficult for Darlene to locate Leonard even as hard labor pains were wracking her body many months later. Shortly after, the two deeply grieving new parents went home without their daughter Rosalynn, whose fragile lungs were unable to sustain life. But it wasn't long before Darlene was a mother-to-be once again.

For a while, life was good. Despite his occasional tomcatting and weekend love affairs with the bottle, Leonard had a steady, solid income. Darlene and the Blossoms were once again in great demand.

Producers such as Lou Adler, Herb Alpert, Lester Sill, and Phil Spector were using them behind such diverse artists as Bobby Darin and Roy Rogers. Their ability to nail any style called for, from gospel to Broadway, made them such a favored group that on occasion, they would do as many as three sessions in a single day. This not only bumped up their exposure but their bank accounts as well. The "Hallelujah!" to this joyous scenario was Darlene giving birth to a healthy baby boy, Marcus Peete.

Eventually, Darlene began doing lead vocal work for Phil Spector, not caring that "He's A Rebel" had been credited on the label to the Crystals … as long as she was paid triple-overtime for the session! The two finally signed a contract, and after "He's Sure The Boy I Love" was released in 1963 (and credited yet again to the Crystals), Phil decided "Darlene Peete" or "Darlene Wright" just wouldn't cut it, so he dubbed her "Darlene Love." It was under that name that Spector released her first credited hit, "(Today I Met) The Boy I'm Gonna Marry." It wasn't until years later that the epic legal battle between the singer and her producer finally wound up with Darlene recouping some of the monies she was owed because of the unscrupulous and highly dubious bookkeeping at the Philles record label.

After the irrevocable split that resulted, Darlene and the Blossoms did a great deal of work behind the Righteous Brothers, with whom they had agreed to tour. Dates in nearby Las Vegas were easily handled because of the short hop between the gambling/entertainment mecca and California, where the Peetes were living, allowing the kids to come along if necessary.

But once everyone went on the road, the Peetes' marriage really began to turn sour. Although Leonard had been dallying around, he became wildly jealous of what his imagination allowed him to believe were Darlene's side affairs. It never mattered that in fact, she never strayed. All the "boyfriends" he fantasized Darlene had ... had become his reality. It all came to a head one evening when the three Blossoms and their spouses went to see Marvin Gaye at a club in Los Angeles.

Marvin had arranged for the three couples to sit right up front, and then made them feel extra-special by playing almost entirely to them. Take a few smiles from the stage ... mix it with all the booze Leonard had consumed ... and take it out to the parking lot where he had dragged Darlene by the hair, convinced that she had something going on with the Prince of Soul. That's where he belted his wife in the face!

Despite her church's doctrine forbidding divorce, that was the turning point. She had had it with her cheating, boozing, body-bashing husband — who had gladly accepted Darlene's earnings while objecting to all the attention being paid to her. After his wife called the cops and had him arrested for slugging her, he apologized with every breath in his body, but it fell on deaf ears. Out the door he went.

Leonard was very humble throughout the divorce proceedings, and Darlene got full custody of their sons Marcus, who was now seven, and Chawn, age four. Although they were divorced, the two remained on very good terms and shared parenting responsibilities to accommodate each other. The court ordered Leonard to pay just $35 in weekly child support, so Darlene now had no choice but to work steadily to provide for her family.

While she no longer had any romantic feelings left for Leonard, Darlene and the boys still shared his life. She often took her sons to watch their dad play football on weekend afternoons. It was on one such Sunday that she met a younger guy named Wesley Mitchell. Having had no romance in her life since her very serious affair with Bill Medley, she had no particular interest in Wesley, but he was very persistent, and after a year, the two began dating. Darlene admits to having been blasé about the whole relationship, which had neither the passion of her days with Medley nor her great physical attraction to Leonard. She accepted Wesley's ring despite feeling that she really didn't love him and that the whole thing would ultimately be doomed. They married in large part because thirty-one-year-old Darlene was lonely and felt that her sons needed a man around the house.

To his credit, Wesley completed college and got a job as a public school security guard. Then surprise, surprise: in the immortal words of the legendary New York Yankee great Yogi Berra, it was "déjà vu all over again"! Just as Leonard has done with ladies he met at work, Wesley, too, began fooling around on the job. Despite a nasty confrontation with one of his girlfriends, Darlene felt her marriage was too new to extricate herself from … and then once again, she found herself pregnant. In 1974, her third son, Jason Davion Mitchell, was born.

There were still problems, of course. Wesley was not only unfaithful; he was also extremely tyrannical with his stepsons, who were approaching their teens. Need it be pointed out that no matter what specific problem arose in the house, the one at fault was never Wesley?

Abuse doesn't have to be physical. While a beat-down may leave both physical and emotional marks on one's psyche, the scars of mental abuse (like the kind experienced by Chuck Negron in the orphanage) can last even longer.

When Jason was still a newborn, Wesley came home one day and told his wife he was taking their son and leaving. Already stunned, Darlene was further shocked by the police, who told her that since the child was taken by his father, the abduction would not be classified as a kidnapping — and that while she could file a missing persons report, the best thing to do would be to just wait it out until Wesley contacted someone.

It took four agonizing, horrendous days before he finally made contact with both sets of grandparents to tell them their grandson was fine, and that neither he nor Jason would be back anytime soon. Desperate for help, Darlene called her dear friend Nancy Sinatra, who passed word of the situation on to her famous father. One did not mess with Frank Sinatra. By the next day, officers had tracked Wesley down and, fearing for his life, he returned the child.

After giving him a number of weeks to think about it, Darlene took her husband back, not having the desire to be divorced for a second time. She was working so often now that being home held no appeal for her, as long as her boys were cared for.

The next decade was a very tough one for Darlene. Two of her sons had brushes with the law, and since many of the folks with whom she had worked previously were past their peak, her participation in their careers was no longer needed. This was partly due to technological advances in recording, which eliminated the need for many of the backup singers who formerly had been critical to a record's success.

As for going out as a solo act: no one knew her name. Sure, the public knew her voice ... but since she hadn't been credited for so much of the work she did with Phil Spector and others, record companies insisted that no one knew who she was. She did a three-day showcase to get the word out, which drew a bunch of supportive friends and many enthusiastic fans to the venue, but her phone remained silent. There were no music executives lining up to sign her to a contract, and so she was home all the time, with the family only able to count on Wesley's income. His cheating continued, as did his constant accusations of Darlene doing something wrong. The final straw came when he defaced the Wrights' family bible.

Despite all she put up with and her repeated attempts to salvage it, this 10-year marriage also ended in divorce. Darlene let out a big sigh of relief to be free of the burden but sadly, down to her last dollars, she knew she'd have to turn to family and friends to help her through this difficult time of unemployment. At one point she found some work...as a housemaid, cleaning other peoples' toilets! She told me there was nothing she wouldn't do to support her kids.

After all the mental and spiritual ordeals she endured, first with Leonard and then with Wesley, Darlene was further insulted ... by her own mother, of all people, who refused to let Darlene and Jason come to live with her. Ellen Wright didn't want any loud child around on the weekends (the only times Darlene had Jason, who was seven by that time), and she claimed she was afraid of how high the electricity bills would run! (Really, Mama?) She used any and every excuse to keep her child and grandson out of her house. Years passed before Darlene could forgive her.

*****

Once Diana Ross left the Supremes, Mary Wilson worked constantly to keep the various combinations of interchangeable talent in the group alive. By the early '70s, their records weren't selling well. When they toured, they were not always the headliners. Dealing with Motown became heartbreakingly tedious. A discouraged Mary was convinced that Berry Gordy and the powers that were now running the company were trying as hard as they could to end the group.

Despite having fifteen songs reach the Billboard R&B chart between 1970 and 1977, only five of them cracked the Top 10, with "Stoned Love" the sole chart-topper, spending one week at #1. They also landed fourteen on the Hot 100, and even had seven songs on the Adult Contemporary Chart between 1970 and 1972.

As depressed as she was, Mary tried to keep her sanity by keeping in touch with family and childhood friends as much as possible. She felt like she was running in place, going nowhere fast. The end of '72 found the Supremes at the Apollo Theater in New York, working with Eddie Kendricks, and receiving the NAACP Image Award as Best Female Group. Despite that, the bottom line seemed to be pointless to Mary, since after the booking agents and Motown deducted what they thought was coming to them, the ladies were left with nothing. They were performing to half-filled rooms, and money was very tight.

At this point, the group's contract with the parent company was coming up for renewal, and Mary could no longer be sure they would be offered a new one. She, Lynda Lawrence, and Jean Terrell started to sense that this might be the time to leave Motown. They worked for a time with Stevie Wonder producing their records, and while Mary tried the best she could to be upbeat and positive, she was starting to take stock of who she really was, and what she wanted to do with her life.

She didn't dwell on it extensively, but she did think about what was missing from her daily existence … specifically, a husband and child. While the 29-year-old Mary didn't fixate on marriage, her mother was constantly reminding her about how great it would be to be a grandmother.

In 1973, the Supremes opened at the Flamboyan Hotel in Puerto Rico, and from the stage, Mary spotted a very attractive man in the audience. After the show, she met Pedro Ferrer in person, and zing went the strings of their hearts! For the next few weeks, they were inseparable. This wealthy, well-dressed, intelligent man swept Mary completely off her feet. Both knew deep in their hearts that they were destined to marry.

With the intention of living together first, Pedro came to Los Angeles for an extended stay. For a while all was fine, but after a few weeks, Mary noticed that her boyfriend was getting a little too bossy with Willie, a young relative she was raising, and was a bit too possessive of her. The longer he stayed, the less sure Mary was about the wisdom of marriage.

Pedro then announced that he was going home — which would have been a perfect time to call the whole thing off, except the physical attraction between them was too strong, and Mary was determined to make it work. Her Supremes group had been kicked to the curb by Motown and she had come to rely on Pedro for love and support to get her through her feelings of failure and vulnerability. She was determined to succeed at love.

One day in the middle of Mary's battle with Berry Gordy over their management and the ownership of the name "Supremes," Pedro showed up with all his belongings ... he was here to stay! Shocked, she let him in — but it wasn't too long before they were arguing again. She wanted him out; he wanted to stay. It came to a head when, in her fury, Mary slapped him. He slapped her back, and the hitting continued. When it was over, he wrote his intended bride a note apologizing and asking for another chance, which he got. It was too difficult for Mary to reject him because she knew his faith and belief in her were genuine and unwavering, and he helped convince her she could accomplish whatever she set out to do.

Her relationship with Motown and the bickering among the Supremes were battles Mary was continuing to fight, but at least she and Pedro were still tight and together 24/7. The two went down to visit his family in Santo Domingo, where she learned how highly respected they were for having played a role in attaining the first free election in the Dominican Republic in nearly forty years.

It was there that the differences between her and her fiancé became even more evident: in his society, men were the bosses, the providers, and were to be shown deference when in public. The wives ruled the roost at home. On the way back to California, the impulse to dump him was strong. She saw clearly how easily she had been roped into the relationship by his great looks and willingness to give; now Mary felt that he was on the taking end, and was smothering her.

Pedro was now permanently in Los Angeles, where he planned to continue law school. Meanwhile, things at home remained difficult. Willie was now fourteen and, like the rest of the family, didn't want Mary to marry Pedro. The teenager was going through a difficult period in his life, and he and his future stepfather were constantly at it; the young man had a problem with Pedro's attempt to control him. Even though she acknowledged to herself that there were a million reasons why her upcoming wedding shouldn't take place, Mary's love — and determination to succeed — wouldn't allow her to call it off.

On the nights she didn't feel like going out, Mary remained home while her fiancé immersed himself in all the abundant nightlife Hollywood had to offer. Everyone he ran into had nothing but nice things to say about Mary — which led him to believe without substantiation, that Mary had slept with some of the men. One night, he stormed into the house, called Mary a whore, and slapped her around once again.

While all this drama was going on at home, things were still in turmoil with Motown, although Mary had hired an outside lawyer to try and straighten things out. The negotiations over a new contract and the use of the name "Supremes" remained problematic, as did who, exactly, would be part of the group. And while Smokey Robinson had promised to produce them, the Supremes hadn't recorded for nearly a year. Mary gave herself a deadline of New Year's Day 1974 to get things in order.

On the road, audiences were relatively sparse, but the abuse from Pedro was not. He kept calling her a prostitute and wouldn't believe that men with whom she may have had a relationship in the past (Duke Fakir, Tom Jones, and others) weren't still sleeping with her. Mary had allowed him to read the diaries she had been pouring her heart into for decades, and he claimed to feel that he knew her much better for having done so. However, that didn't stop him from tearing out pages where there was anything mentioned about a man!

Perhaps the saddest part of this saga was that Mary was blaming herself for the mess she was in, not even considering that perhaps something was wrong with Pedro and his part in the relationship.

Meanwhile, Mary was still battling the label, and when Berry Gordy wouldn't budge, she feared he would get three different singers to perform as the Supremes. She convinced herself that her only chance of survival was to leave Motown, but she was seized by panic every time she thought about what the future would hold if that were to happen. Then, amazingly, Gordy called her and asked her simply what it was that she wanted. She caught her breath and told him she'd like half of the name "Supremes." To her shock, he readily agreed — and against her fiancé's advice, she signed a new contract, grateful that she wouldn't be doomed to poverty. The bulk of her income continued to come primarily from touring rather than record sales. It wasn't until later that Mary read the fine print and realized her new deal wouldn't be worth anything until either the name or Motown itself was sold. That would happen years later, in 1988.

The trio had been booked at the Sahara Hotel in Lake Tahoe for a short engagement, and was then due to take the show to Las Vegas.

She and Pedro, who Mary had begun involving more and more in her business life, decided it would be the perfect time and place to tie the knot.

Her honeymoon was then spent touring in the Far East, with her domineering new husband by her side. Uh oh! Now that he had a ring on his finger, Pedro took over as the boss not only of Mary but also of the group itself. He loved nothing more than playing the big shot, treating everyone to dinner and drinks.

Sick and tired of warring against Motown and kowtowing to Pedro, she started to realize how much her life had changed for the worse. Rather than being proud, optimistic and strong, she now felt like a scared, suspicious coward. Frazzled by the need to watch her every word and move when the two were out socially, Mary pretty much gave up nightlife altogether and stayed home.

Soon she discovered she was pregnant, which thrilled her and her husband until the realization hit that she would not only have to keep working hard and often, but there was now the need for a larger house. In addition to her "son" Willie, Pedro's sister and brother were living with them, and Mary became extremely distressed by the differences between them in parenting styles. By this time, Pedro had left law school and was working as road manager for the act.

Their conflicts were constant, and once more Pedro lost control and beat up his pregnant wife. Mary felt totally smothered and numb. The touring continued, sometimes without Pedro, and his insane jealousy and paranoia continued to mount. So did his attempts to make himself a mover and shaker in Hollywood, by wheeling, dealing, and laying on the charm. Mary knew that she had no choice but to keep on performing. She was in debt over her head, shouldering the burden of supporting not only Pedro, but also all the kids, her mother, and the Supremes.

At this point, it finally hit her that even after all the accolades and awards the Supremes had received through the years, she was the least-known of the original trio — and that as far as record buyers and club goers were concerned, none of the original members were left. She thought about perhaps disbanding the group; the gigs they had been getting were in places out in the middle of nowhere, and the audiences were primarily young kids. She tried to convince herself that she would make it to the top once more, yet going onstage became a fearful experience for her.

At long last, Mary gave birth to a daughter, Turkessa. It entailed major surgery, but the new mother barely had time to rest. Motown was preparing to release *The Supremes* and a tour of Japan was scheduled for just three weeks later.

Sadly, the new baby created a new wedge between Mary and her husband. While most new parents would have been blissfully happy to have an addition to the family, Pedro, who was now officially managing the group, was rarely home. The only interactions between them were fights. The main reason why Mary kept holding on to her husband was her total trust in him, to the exclusion of anyone else. She was completely aware of his many shortcomings but trying to teach him anything was futile. Even during the subsequent performances in Tokyo, Pedro continued his running around at night, and when the two were out in public together, he would constantly insult her. Needless to say, this stoked Mary's insecurities and in fighting to keep his love, she described herself as nearly schizophrenic.

Mary was clearly waging a two-pronged battle at this point: she was fighting desperately to keep the Supremes going while Motown continued to make her life miserable, by basically neglecting the group. She was also working hard to stay married. Pedro had threatened to divorce her and take Turkessa with him, which totally terrified her; she would have done anything to avoid that.

By late summer, Pedro had made headway with some of Motown's top people, especially Suzanne de Passe, who headed the creative division. Of everyone, she put forth the most effort on the Supremes' behalf. Suzanne saw to it that they got good material, the best photographers and other key personnel, and most importantly, she and Pedro worked well together.

The shots in the arm seemed to be working. The Supremes — now consisting of Mary, Susaye Green, and Scherrie Payne — were finally getting positive reviews and they appeared on numerous television shows, but Mary still felt that they weren't getting the support from the label to make the newest incarnation of the group work. Their touring took them to England, where they had always received tremendous fan support and loyalty, as well as to Germany, France, Italy, and Switzerland, where they performed at the Montreaux Jazz Festival. It was here that Pedro showed how much he disliked a sexy dress Mary was wearing by beating her up, leaving her with a black eye just before the group was about to go onstage.

While the overseas tour had been successful, audiences back in the States were much less enthusiastic. Mary and Pedro were living in a mansion in the very upscale Hancock Park section of Los Angeles, and had employed the staff one would expect of a star. The only problem was that such a lifestyle cost big money — and the truth was whatever income they had quickly flown out the window.

Mary knew in her heart that her new Supremes were probably not going to make it big again. Attendances continued to dwindle, and for one show, they had to settle for being an opening act with a mere half-hour allotted for their performance. Mary's personal hell kept getting deeper and darker. She and Pedro were having serious conversations about her going on as a solo act.

By the end of the '70s, Mary knew that she and her spouse were on their way to divorce court, and truthfully, she wasn't in love with him anymore. Professionally, she continued to have faith that she could once again be successful, and relied on Pedro's business acumen, despite Susaye and Scherrie's strong feelings that they didn't need him. The one thing Mary craved more than anything — happiness — just kept eluding her. Even when Pedro informed her that he was going to start dating other women, Mary took a hard look at her situation in life — her home, family, and expenses — and still felt that she needed her husband in her life.

Then there was every performer's worst nightmare. In 1977, the trio signed a contract with promoter Richard Nader to appear in a final Supremes "farewell" concert at Madison Square Garden. The music business had evolved to such a great degree by this time; either you had to be played in heavy rotation on the radio as a contemporary artist and constantly be on television, or you were considered a washed-up oldies act. Despite the new material Mary and her group had developed, she realized the audience considered her the latter when they booed their performance.

As her thirty-third birthday approached, Mary was pregnant again. Three months after their dismal reception at Nader's show, they performed at the famed Drury Theater in London to great accolades, but this was finally it: the very last show. The Supremes ceased to exist. It was up to Pedro to clean up all the related legal work.

As she had threatened multiple times in the past, Mary Wilson was now truly ready to start out as a solo performer. While her husband tied up loose ends, Mary chose two other women to join her in order to fulfill some previously contracted dates in South Africa. Motown was willing to let her bill her act as Mary Wilson *of* the Supremes. When she returned to the states, fully comfortable in her new role as lead singer, she ran into more legal problems with the label regarding the use of the name of the group, and finally had to sue Gordy and the company.

By the time their son Pedro A. Ferrer was born at the end of September 1977, Mary and Pedro were in dire financial straits. After a brief recuperation period, Mary began her solo career in earnest. She chose Karen Jackson and Kaaren Ragland to be her backup singers. Despite deliberate screw-ups with some of her dates and shows that were canceled because Motown was threatening to cut off promoters if they billed Mary using the Supremes' name, she and the ladies performed. After one such show, Pedro stormed into the house after being out all night and not only shoved his wife into the bathroom and smacked her so hard her eyes swelled up immediately, he then grabbed the gun he kept for protection and rubbed it up against Mary's forehead, demanding to know who had been in her bed that night.

That was all she could take! There was no doubt in her mind that divorce was inevitable, but at the same time, she was gaining more and more confidence onstage and realized that her experiences with her abusive husband were teaching her to be a stronger person she needed to be when times were rough.

And rough they were! By early 1978, the couple was in a deep financial hole, and once again Mary went back on the road. To no one's surprise, Motown was making performing extraordinarily difficult because of her use of the name "Supremes." Still, she plugged on.

After a six-week summer tour overseas, during which time Pedro had remained in California straightening out legalities, Mary returned home to an apartment in L.A. The couple had been forced to sell their gorgeous home to make ends meet. When her husband returned from a trip to Mexico, Mary lied to him about a night out she had spent with some friends. This time not only did she get beaten up, but was also threatened with a gun.

Despite the horror she was living with, however, there two bright spots at the time. There was an agreement with Motown that settled some old issues, and talk of a new solo career. Mary was encouraged and excited by the potential to regain her self-esteem and cover herself enough financially to be able to kick Pedro out the door for good.

Ah … but as the old expression goes, man plans and God laughs. Once again, Mary found herself pregnant. Onstage, she was cool and confident … offstage, she felt like she couldn't get any lower. Her Motown contract called for two LP's per year over the next five years, and her self-titled debut album came out in August of 1979 to great reviews and enthusiasm from her fans. She and Pedro had decided to use an English producer for four songs who had had great success with Elton John. Two of them were power ballads, while two had the rough-and-ready sound with which Tina Turner would enjoy such success in the mid-1980s. Unfortunately, the recording was ahead of its time and Motown hated it, wanting only to release dance music.

By the end of that year, the label ushered Mary out the door — but amazingly, Motown gave her back her master tapes! It was the first time they had ever relinquished control of them to an artist. As the decade came to a close, Mary felt stronger than ever and threatened Pedro with a divorce if he didn't get his act together within a year. It was obvious that he didn't feel Mary would ever go through with it, and the violence and aggression, especially during sex, went on unabated.

His humiliation of his wife in front of the kids was the final nail in his coffin for Mary. On New Year's Day 1981, divorce papers were served to a totally unprepared Pedro. Her fears that her soon-to-be ex would jump through hoops to keep the kids turned out to be un-warranted. Mary was finally free. At last, she would now be able to live life on her own terms and concentrate on pumping new life into her career and family.

CHAPTER 8
Why???

It's the eternally unanswerable question: why do bad things happen to good people? Usually, it doesn't even pay to ask. They just do, and unfathomably and irrevocably alter one's life, even if that person is a superstar with millions of people wanting to be in his or her shoes.

Chuck Negron's early years were a child's worst nightmare, leaving him mentally and physically scarred for life.

His family lived in a two-room Bronx walk-up not far from Yankee Stadium and his parents split when he and his sister were very young.

> *My family was broken up when I was four, when my mother and father divorced which back then was rare; now it happens all the time. I would stay home and wander the streets. And we're talking it started in second grade... third grade. And then I left and went to the orphanage. My mother put my sister and*

I in a place called Woodycrest and it was the home for "friendless children." That was their moniker.

And it really is where my life and my psyche and my whole perception of people and love and my role in this world changed. It was a terrible experience. They didn't have the requirements they have now to work in these places. Matter of fact, I think the only requirement was to be a felon. So they had people who put signs on me like "I wet my bed", and they had a sign "He wets his bed" and made me wear it to school. Big sign. If you could picture this: I was very thin, I had one bad eye so they had a patch over my good eye, you know, so the bad eye would get stronger, I wet my bed, so all I didn't have was the sign on my back...you know "Beat Me Up" or something. That's abusive.

It was not long after this that Geraldo Rivera, then an investigative reporter at WABC-TV, did his Peabody Award-winning expose on what was really going on behind closed doors in a local New York facility housing vulnerable children. It was very clear at the time the personnel at such homes were not enlightened enough to care properly for fragile children such as Chuck.

For me as a young, instinctive, sensitive person, so to speak, I knew these people were not qualified to take care of this damaged kid, and I knew they didn't care either. You know, thank God for the ones who were committed to really helping kids, and there were some. But for the most part, they didn't have the skill or even the talent to be in that field. Let alone the training...

I was very scared, and I was very frail. I didn't get big until I was in my teens. I have a twin sister and she was much bigger than me until we were, you know, thirteen or fourteen. I also had that weak eye that went in, and I had corrective shoes. I had problems with my feet.

Everyone around Charlie (as he was called then) branded him a loser, so *their* perception became *his* reality. He thought of himself in the same way. He was also a loner. Nancy was his only savior.

She was in a different area, and she was the one who took care of me. She was my caretaker; she was the one that got up in the middle of the night and walked me to the bathroom, turned on the light for me cause I was afraid to get out of bed, you know. She was the one that helped me with my homework...the only one in my life that ever read me a book.

I was there for a couple of years. But then in, like, the sixth grade I was home again. My mother did come back and pick us up, but by that time the damage was done. I had no idea she was coming back. Anyway, so yeah, I couldn't read or write, so my mom put me in a private school, and within a little over a year, I was almost up to speed. And in junior high school I started doing better and better, and by high school I was fine - although that emotional stigma stays with you. You never feel good enough after that. You just don't feel you're smart enough. And when I went into college it was the first time when I actually did well, and I went, "You know, I can do this."

Singing and basketball, to which he was totally devoted, proved to be this poor, broken child's way out of the darkness…until success turned his life into the darkest shade of black.

*****

There are innumerable personal tragedies that people suffer in their every-day lives. One of the worst imaginable is losing a child. Mary Wilson, Darlene Love, Otis Williams, and Gladys Knight, sadly know this first hand.

In the early 1990s, long after both the original and subsequent Supremes lineups were over and Mary had embarked on a solo career, she decided life for her in Hollywood was no longer what she wanted. She packed up everything and moved to Washington, D.C., but after only one year, she moved her mom and three kids to the edge of the glitz capital of the United States, Las Vegas.

The neighborhood didn't take kindly to the new residents. Her children, Turkessa, Pedro and Rafael - being black teenagers - were viewed as threatening menaces by neighbors, and any time there was an incident of any sort, Mary was sued. After all, she was rich and famous, so why not? The boys' father, from whom Mary was divorced, lived in Los Angeles, so once again Mary packed up and moved. Her eighteen-year-old daughter and her fiancée were in college and stayed in Vegas. Since the boys were still relatively young, they went to live with their dad, and Mary took a small place not far from them. Small is the operative word here. Since she didn't have much space in her new home, Mary figured she'd take some things back to Turkessa and Anthony for their new residence back in the desert. Her son Rafi wanted to come along, so the two of them packed up the car and set out.

They never made it.

> *My son Rafael was fourteen and he died in a car accident...a car that I was driving. It's amazing, as a parent, you know, you always try to protect your children when they go out...you're, like, worried to death. I remember my mother; when we were teenagers and we would go out and come in like eleven o'clock and she'd still be sitting there waiting... like "Why is she sitting there waiting? Everything is fine." You worry about the outside....you worry about other people... what's gonna happen to your children out there? And the biggest part for me, losing Rafi, was that I was the one driving the car.*
>
> *I cannot explain to this day how it went out of control. I really don't know, but it did, and he was thrown from the car. He was wearing a seat belt; I was as well, uh, the door was locked. It was one of those Cherokee Jeeps and they had these locks on the outside of the door so if the car toppled over, then the lock will pop open. And the seatbelt did not hold him; his body was thrown as the car tumbled over many, many times. He sustained a lot of internal injuries and I understand that he was alive for a little while.*

I also sustained internal injuries. But mine, I guess somehow, my body was strong and I lived, but that moment was a very long moment, and when I was told that he was still alive, I knew that my son had died already. It was one of these things where Rafi was... you know how you say as parents you don't have favorite children? But you do. And my other two children always tell me, they say "Mommy, you know Rafi was always your favorite child."

And I have to say "Yes, he was". He was the kind of kid that every time he'd run past me he'd hug me and he'd kiss me and say, "Mommy, I love you, I love you, I love you." And he would always say, "Mommy, I'm only here for you. If it wasn't for you I wouldn't be here."

When we were lyin' there on the ground, I couldn't move. I realized the moment that he left because it was a moment when it seemed like I was about to die and all of a sudden it just sort of switched and I knew that he was gone. And then all those things he'd ever done or said, they made sense. And it was in that moment that I just embraced having had him in my life for fourteen years. And when I got to the hospital, they waited to tell me he had passed, and I told him that I knew. And my daughter said, "How did you know, Mom?" I just knew. My best friends Rita Coolidge and Brenda Russell came out to Barstow where I was and stayed in the hospital for a whole entire week. We sorta celebrated his death that entire week. And it's hard to say to people, and I hope they take this the way I'm giving it, but I just was very, very happy that I had had him in my life. That's what I've always celebrated since he left.

You don't understand...but that's what life is all about. I think there are a lot of things that people in life try to understand, and I think there are some things you just have to accept.

I think any parents who lose a child know exactly that feeling of disbelief. The one thing that I really think helped me was that I had lost Florence [Ballard] prior to that, and learned how to deal with loss. So when I lost my son, I realized the wonderful fourteen years that I had had with him. I was blessed to have known him. And then I thought about there are people that come in and out of your life; they go and they come and they are still there, you just don't see them. So it's almost one of those things where I think in the universe, things are never really lost. They're someplace, you know, and so it brings about our spirituality and basically to me, that's what life is. It's a spiritual thing. I will always have a hole in my heart for Rafi. But I do believe that I'm a happy person - and I can be unhappy about a situation, but it doesn't make me an unhappy person. Life is about discovery. I mean, you can discover good and bad

*things. They're all there. It's about how you can deal
with them and go on and get beyond all of that.*

*****

After Darlene Love joined the Blossoms and their sound was honed, their first professional backup gig was with the teenage idol James Darren, who was then starring on television's *Hawaiian Eye* and would later play Gidget's boyfriend in the movies. They also had the chance to sing behind the silky voice of Sam Cooke.

To keep it all in perspective though, the girls' performances were still primarily at parties and sock hops, leaving them a great deal of time for what Darlene loved the most: being a typical teenager enjoying movies and football games.

Leave it to her to become the envy of all her friends by landing the biggest catch of all: she began dating Leonard Peete - who was three years older, had been a high school football hero and was now working at a grocery store. Before Darlene graduated, Leonard proposed to her. She wasn't sure at all how her family would respond to this, especially her dad. Surprisingly, the greatest opposition she faced came from her mother, who certainly didn't want to lose the family member who served as a maid, cook, and clean-up person, and the one at whom she could direct her temper. Needless to say, that only accelerated her daughter's determination to get out of the house.

Then fate took over as the deciding factor that hastened her plans: she became pregnant. She was four months along when she told her family. To no one's surprise, her mother first ordered her daughter to leave the house but later softened a bit by agreeing to talk about it the next day.

Immediately, Darlene called Leonard, and in the very darkest hours of the morning, and the two of them ran away. They hid out for a few days and finally Leonard's mother, who was more compassionate to their plight, gave her son her blessing to marry his pregnant fiancée. That same day they did their blood tests and tied the knot at City Hall.

While happy to be married, Darlene was melancholy about her new status of wife. She was sad that especially being a preacher's daughter, she didn't have the church wedding every girl dreams of, with family and friends in attendance. Eventually, the Wrights, accepting the reality of what their daughter had done, gave them a lovely, big reception.

She didn't really have time to fall too deep in the doldrums over things, because she and Leonard had to set up house and prepare for their bundle of joy. Even singing became secondary to Darlene. The saddest part of her new life was the realization that dawned shortly after she became pregnant… that her new husband had a wanderlust that he was fulfilling with other women. He wasn't even home the night she went into labor a month before she was due. When he arrived at two o'clock the next morning, he found Darlene hysterical and rushed her to the hospital. He never even took the time to get rid of the evidence in his car that he had been with his latest girlfriend on the beach.

By the time they got to the emergency room Darlene's water had broken and within just a few hours their daughter, Rosalynn, came into the world, weighing six pounds. The new mom became concerned when they didn't bring the infant to her within a reasonable time… a haggard-looking Leonard finally came to his wife's room to tell her their baby had been born with bronchial pneumonia. Being a preemie, Rosalynn's lungs weren't developed well enough to sustain her, and after days in an incubator, she died, despite all the prayers offered by everyone. Riddled with grief, Darlene decided against a funeral and, with the hope that perhaps she would save other parents from what she had gone through, turned her baby's body over to science.

A few months after suffering the heartbreak of coming home without her child, Darlene became pregnant again. She knew the romantic vision she had when she got married was just a mirage, and that her music was her most promising future. After briefly mourning her daughter, she went back on the road. The amazingly successful career she would eventually have wasn't even on her horizon yet.

***

While in his mid-teens, Otis Williams found himself becoming consumed by the rock and roll music from outside his windows...the radios, record players, and live performances at Detroit's Fox Theater. For about a dollar you could hang out all day, watching performances over and over...and over. The lineups were sometimes as long as ten acts, who performed multiple sets each day. Otis became saturated with performers like LaVern Baker, Chuck Berry, Frankie Lyman and the Teenagers, and especially the Cadillacs, whose showmanship knocked him out. He was determined to form his own group - which wasn't too hard in those days, as Detroit was knee-deep in talent - walking the same school halls as he was, or on the next street corner. Someone would be kicked out of a group or leave for some reason, and there were numerous potential replacements waiting in the wings for their opportunity. Otis was so determined to become famous that he opted to leave school and pursue his dreams.

At the same time, he was dating Josephine Rogers, whom he'd been seeing for a couple of years. Much to everyone's chagrin, she became pregnant. Her mother made it very clear that her grandchild was going to be legitimate, and so the young couple "did the right thing" and got married. In June 1961, Otis Lamont came into the world. They all called him Lamont...except for Granny who nicknamed him June. He was adored by his father.

The Williamses tried to make a go of it but living only on Otis' meager income wasn't enough to sustain the relationship, and eventually, they divorced.

Fast forward to 1983: the group had undergone numerous personnel changes and were still going strong, more so on the R&B chart than the Pop and Adult. Though apart, Otis and Josephine remained friends, keeping in touch primarily because of Lamont who lived with his mother. One evening while performing in Atlantic City, a stunned Otis received the news his twenty-three-year-old son, who had been working construction, had fallen three flights from a roof to his death. The numbness, the incredulity of the loss, and the heart-gripping grief has never subsided, let alone gone away.

***

For many years, Gladys Knight was managed by her son Jimmy Newman. Among other accomplishments, he had helped his mom launch Many Roads, a specialty gospel label featuring the music of his mother and other artists. In 1999 Jimmy passed away of heart failure at the age of thirty-six, leaving behind a wife and five children.

As to why such tragedies happen to wonderful people…well, only God knows why, and He ain't talkin'…

CHAPTER 9
Call 9-1-1!

It's so easy to think of ourselves as invulnerable, especially when we're in our youth and haven't yet had to deal with the often harsh realities that come with age, responsibility, and ....well, just living. Sometimes, however, we experience something that strips away all our naïveté and innocence much earlier than we could have anticipated; something that changes our visions of our lives in dramatic and often traumatic ways. Forever.

This was the case with Gladys Knight and Michelle Phillips, both of whom were assaulted while in their teens.

Michelle had gone to New York with John Phillips after she had broken up his marriage to Susie. While she was still legally underage, she and John agreed with her father that rather than run the risk of getting charged under the Mann Act, they should tie the knot. The act had become law in 1910 and prohibited interstate transit of females for "immoral" purposes...in other words, crossing state lines with a minor to have sex. It has been amended by Congress several times since, primarily to curtail prostitution and protect against sexual exploitation of minors.

John was certainly not interested in risking time in the clink just to sleep with Michelle in another state; furthermore, Michelle points out that being *accepted* was a compelling need of hers, and her deepest desire was to become Mrs. John Phillips. This way, they could have sex, sex, and more sex in any state they wanted. Bring it, baby!

The two made it official in Rockville, Maryland on New Year's Eve 1962.

Now they were married and were about to learn how their ideal, unencumbered life would be put to the test. They took to the road, where they were squarely forced to face its realities: successes, disappointments, temptations, and dangers.

Early one evening in 1963 during a stop in Washington, D.C., before the sun went down over the nation's capital, Michelle walked her dog, Pico. When she returned to her hotel room, she sensed someone behind her.

Okay…that's pretty terrifying for anyone…let alone an eighteen-year-old who had always felt secure, and lacked any sense of fear and or had suspicions about what was potentially lurking in the shadows or around corners. When she turned, she was face-to-face with a conservatively dressed man who pretended not to know whose room he was in, while obviously checking out the place to make sure it was otherwise empty. Satisfied that it was only the two of them, he slammed the door shut and lunged at Michelle and started to strangle her. She fought back with everything she had in her to stay conscious, which made her attacker only more enraged. The fight knocked over a lamp and table and the two of them wound up on the floor with him straddling her. He was so strong that Michelle was sure she would slip into unconsciousness.

Do you know the old expression about timing being everything? It was at this moment she saw John coming around the corner, still naked from a shower. Without blinking, he began to beat the intruder to a pulp, and the two wound up in a breezeway near a large group of oblivious sunbathers. The man got away.

The police had been called, and John and Michelle wondered why no one had come to their aid, even though many sitting around the pool said they had seen a man earlier in the day that had been checking all the doors. Sadly at no time had anyone felt the urge to get involved, and that was the official end of the incident. No one back then had ever heard the now-common admonition "If you see something, say something." For Michelle, who while growing up had heard all her father's warnings about the evils that existed regarding strangers; this was a major turning point. Before, they had just been stories; now it was personal. She knew if timing had been otherwise, she would have been raped or dead, strangled by a well-groomed man who would never appear anything but sane and normal to anyone who passed him on the street.

Goodbye to the innocence of a young lady and welcome to a sense of paranoia and suspicion now deeply embedded in a person whose life had previously been happy-go-lucky. She began to have physical reactions if she found herself alone and convulsions if she was in an enclosed space alone with a man.

*****

Gladys Knight was younger than Michelle by a few years when she had a similar life-altering close call.

After her father had moved out, Gladys lived with her mother, brothers, and sister. Her sense of protection was intact, but she was still dealing with the normal fears of adolescence, like being afraid of the dark.

One evening when she was fifteen, Gladys returned home one following a performance of the jazz band with which she was singing. She entered the house cautiously, aware of the stories of rape, break-ins, and vandalism in the area of Atlanta she called home. Exhausted, she decided to call it a night, turned out her bedroom lamp, and fell asleep.

Suddenly she was jolted awake because her feet were freezing. As she tried to get up she couldn't move. Panicked, she realized there was something on her back which was too heavy to push off. Only it wasn't a "something". It was a "someone" who smacked her with his hand and then clamped it down over her mouth ordering her to keep silent.

Somehow she was able to flip herself over and saw the eyes of a dark-skinned man who kept asking her if she was going to scream or not. All she could do was shake her head no. She tasted blood in her mouth, heightening her panic, and was terrified even though she knew she was at home in familiar surroundings with her siblings nearby.

Her assailant kept repeatedly asking if she was going to fight or give in to him. The latter was clearly not an option in Gladys' mind, and as if she had been splashed with cold water, her thoughts crystallized, and she was mobilized into action. Jamming her knee into his groin was enough to make him loosen his hold on her, and she screamed with all the lung power she could muster. The attacker smacked her in her nose which made things worse for him, as the teenager clawed, yelled, and otherwise went berserk, causing her family to come running. Knowing he had to make a quick exit, the guy dove back through the window he's pried open. Bubba and his friend ran after him in hot pursuit, but the assailant had too much of a head start and was never caught.

Gladys didn't get over her mistrust of men quickly. For a long time she made anyone who wanted to enter her room to knock first, and she took to sleeping with a light on. She also made sure every window was locked at night. Having had such a religious upbringing, she learned to place her faith in God to help her weather the crossover from innocence to what she had experienced. As for her relationship with men after the trauma, she explained to me on Kool 96:

> *"You know, amazingly, even with something like that happening in my life, I've always been able to, and I don't want people to feel like I'm being sanctimonious or anything like that, but I've always been able to count on my faith to get me through whatever traumas or trials and tribulations that I have in my life. So yes, there were things that I saw that might have messed with my trust factor as I grew older as far as men were with them anymore."*

In whatever manner Michelle and Gladys were able to use their coping mechanisms during the years that followed, both went on to become supernovas.

CHAPTER 10
Kicked Out Of The Group

Could there be anything more humiliating than being dumped from the group you co-founded and with whom you had enormous success? Probably not. But that's what happened to two of the world's most popular performers of their time.

Michelle Phillips, the free-wheeling spirit who had stolen John away from his first wife in order to become his second, clearly had self-control issues. She was heavily into drugs as was her entire cadre of pals. By the mid-'60s The Mamas & The Papas were strumming and harmonizing their nine Top-40 hits and Baby Boomers were in the midst of their self-actualization experimentation fueled by the confluence of folk music, rock and roll, R&B and drugs. Members of the hippie subculture were becoming more open about their chemically-induced states, often crediting them for deep musical creativity and as a path to the world's deeper truths.

Michelle also had honed her first-rate ability to flirt. It didn't matter that she was married; if someone caught her eye and she felt like it, she'd pursue him. After all, isn't all fair in love and war??

Denny Doherty - whose best friend Cass Elliot had a mad, wild, unconsummated crush on him - fell victim to Michelle's charms while they were living in tents on the beach in St. John. Initially, she hadn't thought of him as anything more than a pal and great addition to the group. However, by the time Cass arrived unexpectedly, (having come especially because of Denny), there was her ostensible best girlfriend, Michelle, carrying on with the Papa she wasn't married to!

Well, not quite "carrying on". In the Virgin Islands there was definitely a lot of flirting going on and just the whole situation was perpetuating this. I mean nobody even batted an eye if they saw Denny and I rolling around, laughing in the sand. It was just a very playful atmosphere. John just didn't think it was going to turn into anything... he didn't think about that. John's mind didn't go there. Denny kissed me once. We were walking back to Duffy's boarding house where we were staying after we got off the beach. And that morning, I sat down with John and I said, "You know, John, I don't think we should live with Denny and with Cass. I think we should move into our own apartment." And he said "Why?" I said, "Because I have to be honest with you. I find myself being very attracted to Denny." And he said, "I wouldn't worry about that Mich. Denny has no interest in you."

In the midst of their now-muddled Caribbean idyll, the group came face to face with a hard truth: they were out of money. Michelle's American Express credit card, the one so famously recalled in the song "Creeque Alley", had been unceremoniously cut in half in St. Thomas, leaving them flat broke. With heavy hearts, they reached the conclusion that the group was over, and it was time to find some "real" work. Cass had taken leave of the islands; the others returned to California, where John, Denny, Michelle and a nephew lived together. They later discovered Cass was in Los Angeles as well. It was there they were introduced to Lou Adler, who listened to their material and signed them to his label, Dunhill Records.

> *Nothing happened* [with Denny] *until after we were signed, until we had a #1 album. That's what made it so difficult. If it had happened before, Cass would have left the group and The Mamas & The Papas probably would have never existed. But it happened when we had a #1 album. "California Dreamin'" had already become a hit, and "Monday, Monday" was flyin' to the top of the charts. So it made it a very, very difficult position for everybody.*

This became even more traumatic after the group won the 1966 Grammy Award for Best Contemporary (R&R) Group Performance (Vocal or Instrumental) for "Monday, Monday"!

> *It was very awkward; I don't deny that. It was very awkward, but we were doing it. By that time, John and I were separated and John and Denny were living together. Cass had her own house, and, you know, everybody was dating other people.*

CLAIRE STEVENS

> *I was dating Gene Clark* [of the folk-rock group the
> Byrds], *which was kind of a mistake, 'cause that re-*
> *ally, really ticked John off.*

Clark sat in the first row of a concert they did in a theater near
Anaheim, happily flaunting his relationship with Michelle by wearing a very loud jacket that no one onstage, especially John, could
fail to notice. Ironically, in another section of the same row was Ann
Marshall, who John happened to be seeing.

> *I guess that his suspicions about whether or not I was dating Gene*
> *were now confirmed, and he was just wildly jealous and upset. I*
> *know John was really mad. I ran out to the parking lot, and he came*
> *after me saying "You are fired!" and I said, "I don't really think you*
> *have the authority to do that, John." And he said, "Oh, you don't?"*
> *Boy, was I wrong!*

The group went out of town and Michelle heard nothing from them
until a few days later, when a legal letter was hand delivered.

> *I got the letter from my husband, my lover, and my*
> *best friend from my attorney saying we don't want*
> *to work with you anymore. Don't call yourself one of*
> *The Mamas & The Papas. You are no longer in the*
> *group: you are out! It was short and sweet and very,*
> *very painful.*

So did the group have the right to dump her?

> *They did because although we had a contract with*
> *Dunhill, we did not have a contract between the four*

152

of us. So, you know, when I got the letter and I called my attorney, Abe Somer, I said, "Abe, what am I gonna do?" He said, "Michelle, I can't talk to you, I represent The Mamas & The Papas, and you're no longer one of them."

It was quite a shock for me to get this letter. Previously, John had said, "You know, Michelle, I gave it all to you and I can take it all away." And so to prove his point, he did. And I had a lot of begging and groveling to do to get back into the group.

The group hired Jill Gibson to replace Michelle.

The whole firing, I think, lasted almost three months, or maybe two months, but it seemed like a lifetime. I was very alone. And I was being denied the one thing that I really, really worked hard for. I missed the group a lot. I missed everybody. It was...you know...my family, and it was tragic. I was doin' a lot of crying. And I was begging to be let back into the group. And finally, it was a culmination of things; I mean it was the audience who wanted to know where I was, because they never attempted to introduce Jill as someone other than me – they wanted to see if they could get away with having Jill on stage and not making any reference to it.

On top of otherwise tormenting Michelle, the group poured salt on her very open, excruciating wound.

There was a billboard on Sunset Boulevard, and they did a photo session where she sat in exactly the same position as I was sitting. That took a lot of guts for them to do that.

And believe me, I had a screaming fit. They did three concerts with her and they tried to pass her off as me. And the fans eventually started saying "Where's Michelle?" And it was an insult to Jill, the fact that they didn't introduce her.

To complicate matters, the newest "Mama" also happened to be Lou Adler's girlfriend.

You know what? He was in a very awkward position, too, because John was pretty much saying, "Look, this is the way it is. And, you know, if you don't like it, that's too bad because I'm the creative genius here and I'm calling the shots. So you either work with Michelle, or you work with me. Take your pick."

Lou chose the group. In a stunned state of shock and despair, Michelle took a little comfort in the support she had.

I was in California and I had my family. My father, my sister and my godmother were there. And I had my childhood friends. But that's not what I wanted. I wanted back in the group, and I wanted to be working again. So I just plotted my course, and I really did believe that they would let me back in as soon as they thought I had suffered enough.

You know, Jill was doing fine. She was a very good singer, probably a better singer than me. It's just that they didn't have that dynamic without me in the group. And you know whether you love me or you hate me, I do create a certain tension and that's what the group was about. That's who we were. And it wasn't John, Cass, Denny and Jill...it was me.

Well, I did come back and we had another good year.

I think it's that we just basically could not work any harder...you know everything we did, everything we recorded, we did in 2 ½ years. And you know, that's an incredible feat. It was just too hard to continue. We didn't have anything left to sing, we didn't have anything more to write about. I'll tell you the truth, the last two years back into the group John and I had a very good time. We had a wonderful marriage those two years. We were making so much money we didn't know what to do with it. We bought a beautiful house in Bel Air and we each bought a brand new Jaguar XKE. Then we did the Monterrey Pop Festival. [They also had their daughter Chynna by then].

Really I think there was so much demand for product, and we were under so much strain to produce more. In fact if we had done what we really wanted to do, which was return to the Virgin Islands and kind of re-group and write some stuff there, I think we could have gone on for a long time.

So why didn't they do just that?

> *Well, the record company wanted us to be just in the*
> *studio. And they were also afraid that we were al-*
> *ways on the verge of breaking up, which of course*
> *was true - that they were kind of priming Cass as a*
> *soloist.*

In 1967, the "Summer of Love," John and the rest of the group, Lou Adler, producer Alan Pariser, and publicist Derek Taylor pulled off in seven weeks what was to become the biggest, most successful pop event up to that time. Gathering artists from all over the globe, the Monterrey Pop festival featured established acts such The Mamas and The Papas, who closed the last night of the three-day event, Simon & Garfunkel, the Byrds, and the Jefferson Airplane. It also introduced tens of thousands of fans to relatively new acts such as Otis Redding, whose prior performances were mainly in front of black audiences, and The Who. This was also the first time a vast audience was introduced to Ravi Shankar, Janis Joplin, and Jimi Hendrix.

Numerous other acts, including the Beach Boys, the Beatles, Donovan, the Kinks, Eric Clapton and the Rolling Stones, were unable to perform for various reasons. The festival was to become the template for the Woodstock Music & Art Fair, which would follow two years later.

Michelle, John, Denny, and Cass would continue to perform for a while getting totally wrapped up in the druggy, mystical, free-style living that pervaded Hollywood. They were living large and loving every second of it.

However, the group disbanded in 1968 – until it was discovered that they still owed their label an album, which failure to record would be considered a breach of contract. In November 1971, they released *People Like Us* – which Michelle reportedly characterized as sounding "like what it was, four people trying to avoid a lawsuit." It peaked at #84 on the Billboard album chart.

So that was the end of the Mamas and the Papas.

Michelle went on to have a very brief marriage to actor Dennis Hopper in 1970 and became a successful actress, best known for her role as Anne Matheson on *Knots Landing.* Cass Elliot died in 1974 at age thirty-two from a heart attack; despite the persistent urban myth, her autopsy showed no evidence of a sandwich or any other food in her throat or trachea. Heart failure took John Phillips in 2001 at age sixty-five, just two months after he finished recording his final album, *Phillips 66* - and six years later, Denny passed away at his home in Mississauga, Ontario, at age sixty-six.

*****

Chuck Negron also faced the ignominy of being kicked out of his group, Three Dog Night. It was drugs that killed his role in the world of rock and roll and came perilously close to killing him as well. He had headed west to California after receiving an athletic scholarship to a community college in Santa Maria. He had also been singing with a band called the Sorenson Brothers when he was signed to Columbia Records as a solo artist. Eventually, he decided to quit basketball and devote his time to his music.

By the middle of the '60s, the American culture was in midst of a huge transition: the British Invasion was in full swing and a new folk-rock sound was being ushered in to compete with it. This wasn't great news for Chuck since the record label had been grooming him to be a crooner, à la Johnny Mathis. The basketball star/ budding singer packed his bags and headed back home to the Bronx - where he discovered that marijuana, heroin and even the cough syrup Romilar had taken hold among his old pals. Chuck wanted no part of that and headed back to Los Angeles with hopes of getting involved in the club scene.

The scene he did get involved with was not what he had planned. At a party at Donovan's house one night, intoxicated by this great new music scene he was experiencing, he realized what had turned him off in New York now seemed like a good idea...at least the Romilar part. After all, here he was in a free-swinging, drug-addicted culture that he found he liked, so why not?

> *You know it's a very interesting phenomenon, the '60s, where, you know, we just wanted to change things; a lot of drugs were coming in with LSD and then of course, you know, pot. We're doing all these drugs. And back then...people don't know this...but cocaine was non-addicting as far as the doctors were concerned. So yeah, I just wanted to be a part of it all. I was at a party with Janis Joplin, Jimi Hendrix, and everyone... there were all the beautiful young girls... getting high, and I just left college with my shorts and button down shirts. You know, I think they thought I was a narc! I was off and running because everyone used, and since I was an obsessive person, next thing you know, I'm a drug addict.*

It didn't take long for that to happen. Within weeks of his first high, friends with whom he had been taking the drugs became worried about him. Soon he was dropping acid on a regular basis even though he greatly feared the result could only be death. So he stopped the LSD but continued taking mescaline, pot, and peyote - whatever he could score. The 24/7 hippie party scene on the Sunset Strip, with its bars and clubs, hot chicks and music had Chuck in its grasp... and he loved it. When Uncle Sam called him for duty in 1967, he turned to drugs to get out of the draft. It worked.

His contract with Columbia Records came to an end, but Chuck continued pursuing his music career in earnest, even taking a job one summer performing in a series of shows for Job Corps participants in the Pacific Northwest. He didn't make any money, but he did get free room and board. Once home again following the tour, he got wind that Danny Hutton wanted to get in touch with him. After hearing the harmonies of Chuck, Danny, and Cory Wells, the Beach Boys' Brian Wilson, a friend of Danny's, produced a couple of songs for them – until some of his own bandmates objected. They thought Brian was giving away hit songs! (After the trio's contributions were scrubbed, one of the tunes eventually appeared as the Beach Boys' "Darlin'"). By late 1968, the original group had expanded to seven members: Chuck, Danny, Cory, Jimmy Witherspoon, Joe Schermie, Floyd Sneed, and Michael Allsup. Three Dog Night was on the map.

The story of the group's genesis has been told in a previous chapter, but the ousting of one of the founding members has not. It's really a very short epic. Drugs were rampant in this haze of pop festivals, concert tours, and a string of one-night stands that took rock acts from coast to coast. New and additional dangerous drugs found their way into Chuck's body: Seconals, coke, Quaaludes…there were never enough…more! More! MORE!!! Then came the shaking… the falling…the stumbling… the broken bones…the hole in his septum and the black in his lungs. He developed hepatitis and discovered cotton in his blood from using syringes. There were many lost days and nights and non-stop sexual escapades, even through marriages and children! The situation got so bad that the band members took over control of his drugs, dispensing them to him rather than leaving them so he could self-medicate.

By the end of the 1960s, the guys had solidified their standing as one of the seminal rock groups in the country. They first hit the Billboard Hot 100 at the end of 1969 with "Try A Little Tenderness" from their eponymous debut album. That was followed up by "One", "Easy To Be Hard", Eli's Coming", and "Celebrate". In the summer of 1970, Randy Newman's tune "Mama Told Me (Not To Come)" became their first chart-topper, and eight months later, they had their second, "Joy To The World." By then, everyone around the world knew that Jeremiah was a bullfrog! They also made inroads on the Adult Contemporary chart, starting out with "Out In The Country" and then reached #1 with "An Old Fashioned Love Song" and "Black & White". During their first six years of existence, the group scored twelve consecutive gold albums (for total sales of more than sixty million units) and twenty-one straight Top-40 singles.

More than once, Chuck missed shows, was arrested, and prowled the streets of Los Angeles. He crashed and burned numerous times, and was in and out of rehab and hospitals. After spending three weeks in one hospital, where his condition outraged doctors, he was advised that if he continued touring, he would almost certainly die. Often, neither the band nor his then-wife Julia knew where he was.

It's important to clarify that it wasn't just Chuck who was living life in a completely altered state; it would have been very difficult to find anyone involved in the music scene, especially performers, who weren't involved in booze, drugs, and mindless sex to one degree or another. The hallmarks of the psychedelic era, from Chuck's viewpoint, was the writing on the wall for the group - especially the drugs.

> *It probably was the one most powerful reason the band ended in '77. Danny left, I think, in '76. Floyd and Michael and Joe Schermie were among the first to go. Drugs and alcohol devastated that band. It devastated it. You know…everything was changing, everything was new. Everyone was smokin' pot or doin' acid…and, you know, you just kind of want to be a part of it…and if you're predisposed to addiction, you're in major, major trouble. Not everyone had a problem in the band, but a couple guys for sure.*

> *I was one of them; I only can really talk about myself. But it was a tough time because it was so successful and we didn't even know we were in trouble. Then little by little, you know, one guy goes 'cause he can't continue anymore and he's replaced and you go, "Wow, that was drugs, I know that was." Then all of a sudden it becomes crystal-clear that the information you've been given is poor information: drugs don't help you be more creative. Matter of fact, drugs*

steal that from you. And that's something I tell the kids today. They go, "Man doesn't it really make you more creative?" and I go, "Look, I don't think you could save Jimi Hendrix, and River Phoenix, and these guys aren't very creative any more. You know, no, it steals your life is what it does."

Besides drugs, [the Elton John/Bernie Taupin tune] *"Lady Samantha" was one of the dissentions that started separating the band. Because I had had "One" as a Cashbox #1 song and a million-seller, and I had "Easy To Be Hard" in the can and the record company was going "This is another hit." When I picked "Lady Samantha" which was played to me by Gabriel Meckler who was producer of Steppenwolf (who did "Born to Be Wild"), he brought it to me and said, "This is great." Danny went nuts. And he said "Why is Chuck getting all the songs?"* [Meckler responded], *"Well, first of all, Chuck brings a lot of songs, so I'm bringin' one to him." And we ended up really breaking the song up and the song lost its importance. Because what you do is, you compromise you know. I sang lead, but we shared more parts than we should've. Because what happens, and Claire, you made a great point earlier of why the band was together, and what it was, we brought three different identities. It is hard for people to stick with what they do best when one of their peers is havin' all the hits. They want to do what you're doing.*

Hence, the rift which threatened Chuck's continuation in the band. Three Dog Night had called it quits for the first time in 1976, and re-formed in the early '80s. During that period, Chuck wound up in rehab again.

In 1981, Danny and Cory surprisingly proposed a deal to Chuck. With his dad at his side in the meeting, Chuck carefully read both the written words and those between the lines. There was a clause in the contract that assured the band would not be sabotaged by his drug addiction. It also included wording regarding his need for rehab and the conditions under which he could be fired due to incapacitation. If he were to sign, it had to be there and then, without the benefit of any legal guidance.

It was clear to Chuck what this was about: payback…a way to get him out of the band for good and deny him further use of the group's name. They tried to persuade his father that signing the deal would be for his son's own good. The senior Negron, who had no idea of the depth of his son's addiction, saw this as an opportunity for Chuck to get back to work and make more money. Embarrassed by the unspoken truths between him and his dad, and wanting to get this over with as quickly as possible, he signed on the dotted line, knowing instinctively he would be forced out and wind up with nothing.

Shortly thereafter, the Three Dog Night was back performing again, although within a few years the façade again began to crack, and members either left or were fired. Predictably, all that could possibly continue to plague Chuck, did. He even spent time in jail. Finally, it all came to the climactic moment Chuck had always known was inevitable.

On December 10, 1985, their road manager John Meglen was given the unpleasant task of hand- delivering a brief, three-sentence letter from the others, firing Chuck because of the multiple missed performances and the death grip his addiction had on him. Cory and Danny booted his ass. He was history as far as the original Three Dog Night was concerned.

So what, in Chuck's mind, was the bottom line of the breakup?

> *You know, I think probably it was alcohol and drugs and a schedule that was unrelenting. This band did two albums a year and toured at least 210 days. We literally got off the road and went to the studio and it was an amazing schedule. You know it was nuts. But the thing was, I actually went to the manager and I said "This band is being killed here. We need to do something. We need to take a break." And it just wasn't in the agenda, and actually we found out years later that because of the drugs and alcohol, they thought some of us weren't going to make it, so they wanted us to work as long as we could until one of us died. That's the kind of hardball that goes on in the music business.*

However, his career, as history shows, was far from over. He finally kicked the habit and became a very successful artist who still records and performs with The Negron Band to this day. He has released six solo albums so far, and in the summer of 2017, his seventh album dropped, arguably the one that brought him the greatest joy of his recording career. *Negron Generations* featured his daughters Charlotte Rose ("Charlie") and Annabelle Quinn, as well as some previously unreleased Three Dog Night tracks. He has also recently published the latest version of his book *Three Dog Nightmare*, performs in the Happy Together tours with other artists during the summer, and continues to speak out on the hazards and horrors of drug use.

Sadly, the group on the cover of the July 14, 1972 issue of *Rolling Stone* magazine will never be able to stage a reunion concert. Keyboardist Jimmy Witherspoon passed of melanoma in March of 2015, and Cory Wells died seven months later after a battle with multiple myeloma. Chuck's twin sister and champion, Nancy Negron Dean lost her battle with cancer in 2013.

A HUGE THANK YOU....

...to my family...Keith, Lisa and Marc...for their incredible love, support and suggestions as this story progressed...

...to Anita Bonita, who took a bunch of words and unsettled phrases and edited them into coherent readable prose...

...to John Bell, who lit the match that started the fire which got me started writing this book over ten years ago... it's a privilege to call you my friend...

...to Scott Shannon, who heard my voice all those years ago and started me on this incredible journey... I treasure your support and friendship through the years...

BIBLIOGRAPHY
AND SOURCES

The prime source of material for this book was a series of interviews I conducted and recorded with Neil Sedaka, Ellie Greenwich, Chuck Negron, Gladys Knight, Otis Williams, Mary Wilson, Michelle Phillips, and Darlene Love. Their exact quotes appear in italics.

Books:

Benjaminson, Peter. *The Lost Supreme: The Life Of Dreamgirl Florence Ballard.* Chicago: Chicago Review Press, 2009.

Brown, Mick. *Tearing Down The Wall Of Sound: The Rise And Fall Of Phil Spector.* New York: Vintage Books, 2008.

Emerson, Ken. *Always Magic In The Air: The Bomp And Brilliance Of The Brill Building Era.* New York: Penguin Books, 2006.

Fong-Torres, Ben. *The Motown Album: The Sound Of Young America.* New York: St. Martin's Press, 1990.

Hyatt, Wesley. *The Encyclopedia Of Daytime Television.* New York: Billboard Books, 1997.

Knight, Gladys. *Between Each Line Of Pain And Glory: My Life Story.* New York: Hyperion, 1997.

Lazell, Barry, with Dafydd Rees and Luke Crampton (editors). *Rock Movers & Shakers: An A To Z Of The People Who Made Rock Happen.* New York: Billboard Publications, Inc., 1989.

Leiber, Jerry, and Mike Stoller. *Hound Dog: The Leiber And Stoller Autobiography.* New York: Simon & Schuster, 2010.

Love, Darlene, with Rob Hoerburger. *My Name Is Love: The Darlene Love Story.* New York: William Morrow, 1998.

McNeil, Alex. *Total Television, 4th Edition.* New York: Penguin Books, 1996.

Medley, Bill, with Mike Marino. *The Time Of My Life: A Righteous Brother's Memoir.* Boston: Da Capo Press, 2014.

Negron, Chuck. *Three Dog Nightmare: The Continuing Chuck Negron Story.* Indianapolis: Literary Architects, 2008.

Negron, Chuck, with Chris Blatchford. *Three Dog Nightmare: The Chuck Negron Story.* Los Angeles: Renaissance Books, 1999.

Nite, Norm N. *Rock On Almanac: The First Four Decades Of Rock 'n' Roll – A Chronology.* New York: Harper & Row, 1989.

O'Neil, Thomas. *The Grammys For The Record*. New York: Penguin Books, 1993.

Phillips, Michelle. *California Dreamin': The True Story Of The Mamas And The Papas*. New York: Warner Books, 1986.

Podolsky, Rich. *Neil Sedaka: Rock 'N' Roll Survivor: The Inside Story Of His Incredible Comeback*. London: Jawbone Press, 2013.

Ribowsky, Mark. *The Supremes: A Saga Of Motown Dreams, Success, And Betrayal*. Cambridge: Da Capo Press, 2008.

Romanowski Bashe, Patricia and Holly George-Warren (editors). *The Rolling Stone Encyclopedia Of Rock & Roll, Revised And Updated For The 21st Century*. New York: Touchstone, 2001.

Sedaka, Neil. *Laughter In The Rain: My Own Story*. New York: G.P. Putnam's Sons, 1982.

Selvin, Joel. *Here Comes The Night: The Dark Soul Of Bert Berns And The Dirty Business Of Rhythm & Blues*. Berkeley: Counterpoint Press, 2014.

Strong, Martin C. *The Great Rock Discography, Sixth Edition*. Edinburgh: Canongate Books, Ltd., 2002.

Stuessy, Joe. *Rock & Roll: Its History And Stylistic Development*. Englewood Cliffs: Prentice Hall, 1990.

Whitburn, Joel. *Joel Whitburn Presents Hot R&B Songs 1942–2010, 6th Edition*. Menomonee Falls: Record Research Inc., 2010.

_____. *Joel Whitburn Presents The* Billboard *Hot 100 Charts: The Eighties.* Menomonee Falls: Record Research Inc., 1991.

_____. *Joel Whitburn Presents The* Billboard *Hot 100 Charts: The Seventies.* Menomonee Falls: Record Research Inc., 1990.

_____. *Joel Whitburn Presents The* Billboard *Hot 100 Charts: The Sixties.* Menomonee Falls: Record Research Inc., 1990.

_____. *Joel Whitburn Presents The* Billboard *Pop Charts 1955–1959.* Menomonee Falls: Record Research Inc., 1992.

_____. *Joel Whitburn's Bubbling Under The Hot 100 1959–1985.* Menomonee Falls: Record Research Inc., 1993.

_____. *Joel Whitburn's Hot Dance/Disco 1974–2003.* Menomonee Falls: Record Research Inc., 2004.

_____. *The* Billboard *Albums, 6th Edition.* Menomonee Falls: Record Research Inc., 2006.

_____. *The* Billboard *Book Of Top 40 Albums, Revised & Enlarged 3rd Edition.* New York: Watson-Guptill Publications, 1995.

_____. *The* Billboard *Book Of Top 40 Hits, 9th Edition.* New York: Billboard Books, 2010.

_____. *Joel Whitburn's Top Adult Contemporary 1961–2001.* Menomonee Falls: Record Research Inc., 2002.

_____. *Joel Whitburn's Top Pop Singles, 12th Edition.* Menomonee Falls: Record Research Inc., 2009.

Williams, Otis, with Patricia Romanowski. *Temptations, Updated Edition.* New York: Cooper Square Press, 2002.

Wilson, Mary, and Patricia Romanowski. *Dreamgirl & Supreme Faith: My Life As A Supreme (Updated Edition).* New York: Cooper Square Press, 2000.

Articles:

"$2000 Winner." *Jet Magazine*, July 17, 1952.

Bagley, Jim. "Chuck Negron On Second Chances And Life After Three Dog Night." *Goldmine Magazine*, February 18, 2005.

Browne, David. "Darlene Love: Let Love Rule." *Rolling Stone*, June 20, 2013.

Fong-Torres, Ben. "Three Dog Night: See How They Run." *Rolling Stone*, September 14, 1972.

Gilmore, Mikal. "Bob Dylan, The Beatles, And The Rock Of The Sixties." *Rolling Stone*, August 23, 1990.

Hopkins, Jerry. "The Rolling Stone Interview: Cass Elliot." *Rolling Stone*, October 26, 1968.

Katsilometes, John. "Gladys Knight: Performing At Trop Was 'A Dream Come True,' But Staying Didn't Make Financial Sense." *Las Vegas Sun*, September 23, 2011.

Kloman, William. "Sink Along With Mama Cass." *Esquire*, June 1969.

Larsen, Peter. "Three Dog Night's Danny Hutton Talks Music And Fame, Then And Now." *Orange County Register*, July 27, 2012.

Marshall, Ryan. "Darlene Love, From Backup To Center Stage." *Frederick News-Post*, October 5, 2017.

McNair, James. "Michelle Phillips: Trip Of A Lifetime." *The Independent*, October 29, 2004.

Myers, Marc. "The Dixie Cups And 'Chapel Of Love.'" *Wall Street Journal*, June 16, 2015.

Palmer, Robert. "The 50s: A Decade Of Music That Changed The World." *Rolling Stone*, April 19, 1990.

Pareles, Jon. "Stop! In The Name Of Nostalgia." *New York Times*, April 5, 2000.

Rule, Sheila. "The Pop Life: Soundtrack For A Soap." *New York Times*, February 16, 1994.

Sharp, Ken. "A Chat With Michelle Phillips Of The Mamas And The Papas." *Rock Cellar*, May 6, 2016.

Sheff, David, and Martha Smilgis, "In the Latest Mamas and Papas' Saga, Michelle Phillips Says Her Ex, John, Stole His Own Son." *People*, December 10, 1979.

Torem, Lisa. "Darlene Love Interview." *Pennyblackmusic Magazine*, November 25, 2015.

Townson, Drew. "Bones Howe: Elvis Presley, Tom Waits, The 5th Dimension, The Mamas And The Papas And More..." *Tape Op*, March/April 2008.

Tramontana, Gianluca. "Family Toasts John Phillips' 66th." *Rolling Stone*, August 28, 2001.

Weber, Bruce. "Ellie Greenwich, Pop Songwriter, Dies At 68." *New York Times*, August 26, 2009.

Weller, Sheila. "California Dreamgirl." *Vanity Fair*, December 2007.

Websites:

Allmusic.com
Amazon.com
Ancestry.com
BET.com
Casselliot.com
Chucknegron.blogspot.com
Chucknegron.com
Classic.motown.com
Discogs.com
Elliegreenwich.com [archived]
Emmys.com
Forums.stevehoffman.tv
Gladysknight.com
Grammy.com

Hancockcollege.edu

History.com

IBDB.com

IMDB.com

Johnbathke.com

Knotslanding.net

Marywilson.com

Montereyinternationalpopfestival.com

Music-illuminati.com

Neilsedaka.com

Nobelprize.org

Officialcharts.com

Originalamateurhour.com

Oscars.org

Otiswilliams.net [archived]

Rockhall.com

Soulfuldetroit.com

Temptationsofficial.com

The60sofficialsite.com

Theconcertdatabase.com

Thehistorymakers.org

Treatment4addiction.com

Vocalgroup.org

Vulture.com

Wikipedia.org

Wreckingcrew.tv

CLAIRE
STEVENS

Claire Stevens has been a media personality for over thirty-five years.

She was a member of the original Morning Zoo Crew on New York's award-winning radio station Z-100, and has been heard in numerous other formats, including smooth jazz on the SONY Worldwide Network, oldies, album rock, and talk radio. She also was a correspondent for a national internet morning prep service, and was seen as a news anchor for FOX-5 TV in New York City.

She is President of the Triumph Radio Network, and has written and hosted several nationally syndicated programs, including *Streisand Coast-to-Coast*, *The Make Believe Ballroom*™, and *Rockin' Back*™. Claire also served as the President of the New York Board of the National Music Foundation, chaired nationally by the late Dick Clark.

She lives in Westchester County, New York with her husband.

CPSIA information can be obtained
at www.ICGtesting.com
Printed in the USA
LVHW090625181219
640669LV00008B/575/P